# ROMAN RELIGION

This book provides an introduction to the religion and religious practices of ancient Rome. Examining sites that are familiar to many modern
tourists, Valerie Warrior avoids imposing a modern perspective on the
topic by using the testimony of the ancient Romans to describe traditional Roman religion. The ancient testimony re-creates the social and
historical contexts in which Roman religion was practiced. It shows,
for example, how, when confronted with a foreign cult, official traditional religion accepted the new cult with suitable modifications. Basic
difficulties, however, arose with regard to the monotheism of the Jews
and Christianity. Carefully integrated with the text are visual representations of divination, prayer, and sacrifice as depicted on monuments,
coins, and inscriptions from public buildings and homes throughout the
Roman world. Also included are epitaphs and humble votive offerings
that illustrate the piety of individuals and that reveal the prevalence of
magic and the occult in the lives of the ancient Romans.

Valerie M. Warrior is a scholar of Greco-Roman history and religion.
She has taught at a number of North American colleges and universities
and is the author of *The Initiation of the Second Macedonian War* and *Roman
Religion: A Sourcebook*.

# CAMBRIDGE INTRODUCTION TO ROMAN CIVILIZATION

Cambridge Introduction to Roman Civilization is a program of books designed for use by students who have no prior knowledge of or familiarity with Roman antiquity. Books in this series focus on key topics, such as slavery, warfare, and women. They are intended to serve as a first point of reference for students who will then be equipped to seek more specialized scholarly and critical studies. Texts in these volumes are written in clear, jargon-free language and will integrate primary texts into a synthesis that reflects the most up-to date research. All volumes in the series will be closely linked to readings and topics presented in the Cambridge Latin Course.

# ROMAN RELIGION

VALERIE M. WARRIOR

CAMBRIDGE
UNIVERSITY PRESS

# CAMBRIDGE
## UNIVERSITY PRESS

University Printing House, Cambridge CB2 8BS, United Kingdom

One Liberty Plaza, 20th Floor, New York, NY 10006, USA

477 Williamstown Road, Port Melbourne, VIC 3207, Australia

314-321, 3rd Floor, Plot 3, Splendor Forum, Jasola District Centre, New Delhi - 110025, India

79 Anson Road, #06-04/06, Singapore 079906

Cambridge University Press is part of the University of Cambridge.

It furthers the University's mission by disseminating knowledge in the pursuit of education, learning and research at the highest international levels of excellence.

www.cambridge.org
Information on this title: www.cambridge.org/9780521532129

© Cambridge University Press 2006

First published 2006
Reprinted 2016

*A catalogue record for this publication is available from the British Library*

*Library of Congress Cataloging in Publication data*
Warrior, Valerie M.
Roman religion / Valerie M. Warrior.
p.   cm. – (Cambridge introduction to Roman civilization)
Includes bibliographical references.
ISBN 0-521-82511-3 (hardcover) – ISBN 0-521-53212-4 (pbk.)
1. Rome – Religion.   I. Warrior, Valerie M.   II. Series.
BL803.W37   2006
292.07 22–pcc        2005023912

ISBN  978-0-521-82511-5  Hardback
ISBN  978-0-521-53212-9  Paperback

# CONTENTS

———

# ILLUSTRATIONS AND MAPS

## ILLUSTRATIONS

## MAPS

# PREFACE

This book offers an introduction to the religion of ancient Rome through the early second century CE, using a selection of different kinds of ancient testimony to portray Roman action and opinion in areas that they or we would call "religion" – literary texts, epigraphic and numismatic evidence, together with visual representations of surviving artifacts. No background in Roman history is assumed, but readers are urged to consult the revised third edition of the *Oxford Classical Dictionary,* ed. Simon Hornblower and Antony Spawforth (2003), which contains articles by the foremost scholars of Roman religion and history.

The commentary on the ancient testimony is organized thematically and more or less chronologically within each theme. Putting these various sources together, however, does not produce a picture of Roman religion at any specific time but rather a patchwork of disparate sources of different dates. "Consider the source" is a maxim that must be constantly kept in mind. The traditional date of the foundation of Rome is 753 BCE, but the Roman literary sources date no earlier than the late third century BCE. Many of the stories concerning early Roman religion derive from authors writing several centuries after the events they purport to describe. First we must ask: who is the author, in what genre is he writing, when did he live, and how far removed in time is he from the events he is describing?

Inscriptions and coins offer evidence that is more or less contemporaneous with the event described or commemorated. Epitaphs from tombs yield valuable information about the lives of ordinary people who would not otherwise have found their way into the history books. The physical remains of temples, shrines, and altars frequently bear representations of religious ceremonies with details of various rituals that supplement the information given in the literary sources. Votive offerings, such as mass-produced figurines or models of various parts of the human body, give insight into the religious practices of the poorer classes of society.

Roman religion is very different from most of the contemporary religions with which we are familiar. Thus there is a risk of being influenced by our own preconceptions about the components of a religion. For instance, an ethical element is generally absent. As Cicero (106–43 BCE) remarks, when the Romans wanted to be informed about what was morally right, what was morally wrong, and what was neither one nor the other, they turned to philosophers for answers, not to diviners, whose task was to interpret the will of the gods (*On Divination* 2.10–11).

Divination, seeking the gods' will through the interpretation of signs believed to have been sent by them, reflects a natural human desire to ascertain the future, especially in times of crisis and uncertainty. The Romans were no exception to this generalization. Numerous literary references attest to the presence of seers, soothsayers, and prophets, all eager to serve both the state and private individuals. The gods' will was sought before initiating any public business either in Rome itself or abroad. The different signs by which the gods were thought to reveal their will included thunder, lightning, the behavior of birds, the observation of the entrails of sacrificial victims, unusual phenomena such as monstrous births, the interpretation of dreams, prophecies, oracles, and the drawing of lots (Cicero, *On Divination* 1.3 and 12).

A contemporary non-Roman perspective on Roman religion is given by Polybius (c. 200 BCE–c. 118 BCE), a Greek politician who became a historian when he was a hostage in Rome. He observed that *deisidaimonia* – fear and respect for the supernatural – held the Roman state together (Polybius 6.56). The approximate Latin equivalent of the

Greek *deisidaimonia* is *religio,* defined by Cicero as the *cultus deorum,* tending the worship of the gods (*On the Nature of the Gods* 2.8). For the Romans, *religio* was not a matter of faith or belief, of doctrine or creed, but rather of worship – of divination, prayer, and sacrifice. The aim was pragmatic: to avoid the anger of the gods, and to secure their favor.

# ACKNOWLEDGMENTS

I am grateful to Beatrice Rehl for inviting me to write this book and for her generous support throughout the project. To Rachel Rosenweig, who handled the permissions, my thanks go for making the process painless and exciting. It has been a pleasure to work with the entire team at Cambridge University Press.

My colleagues in ancient history deserve much credit, especially Ernst Badian, Kathleen Coleman, and Jerzy Linderski. Alexander G. McKay and the late Lily Ross Taylor stimulated my interest in Roman religion when I was a graduate student.

The book is dedicated to my husband Thomas Stone.

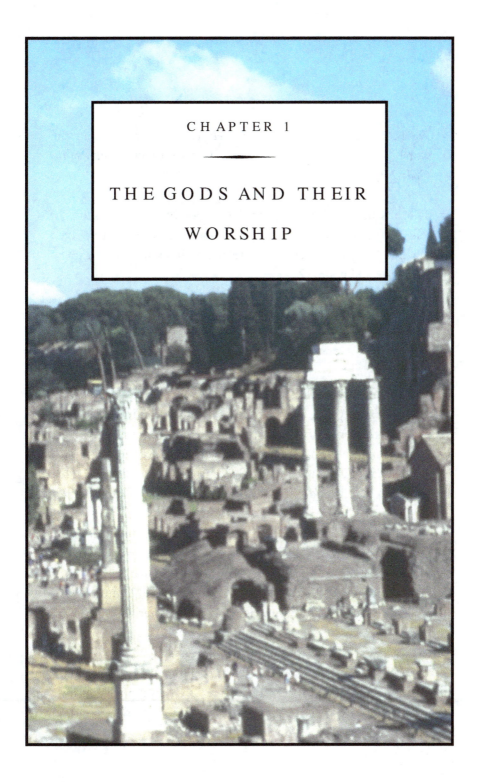

CHAPTER 1
—
THE GODS AND THEIR
WORSHIP

We Romans are far superior in *religio,* by which I mean the worship of the gods (*cultus deorum*). (Cicero, *On the Nature of the Gods* 2.8)

There is no place in our city that is not filled with a sense of religion (*religiones*) and the gods. There are as many days fixed for annual sacrifices as there are places in which they can be performed. (Livy 5.52)

R uins of ancient temples, interspersed among the excavated remains of the ancient city, still bear witness that Rome was indeed a city filled with gods and a sense of religion. Prominent among the remains in the Roman Forum are the temples of Castor, Saturn, Vesta, and the deified emperor Antoninus Pius and his wife Faustina. Overlooking the Roman Forum is the Capitoline Hill, the site of the temple of Jupiter the Best and Greatest. In the area of the Forum Holitorium near the river Tiber, the modern tourist can see ancient columns incorporated into a side wall of the church of San Nicola in Carcere. In the Campus Martius area, the emperor Hadrian's reconstruction of the Pantheon stands in all its grandeur amid the hustle and bustle of contemporary Rome, still bearing the inscription commemorating its original builder, Marcus Agrippa, who was a close associate of the emperor Augustus. The building was consecrated as a Christian church in the seventh century CE, another example of continuity and change within religious traditions. These and many other temples and shrines, dedicated to a multiplicity of different deities, were located in the busiest areas where the civic, commercial, and legal business of the city was conducted.

1. Roman Forum and Palatine Hill from the Tabularium, with the Arch of Septimius Severus at the lower left, the Arch of Titus in the distance, and three columns of the Temple of Castor on the right. (The very late Column of Phocas, early seventh century CE, is in the foreground.)

2. The church of S. Nicola in Carcere, Rome, which incorporates elements of three Roman temples that were originally on this site in the ancient Forum Holitorium (vegetable market): (a) facade (b) ancient columns in the sidewall.

3. The Pantheon, Rome: exterior, showing the facade, dome and, above the columns of the facade, the inscription naming Marcus Agrippa, who built the original Pantheon in his third consulship, 27 BCE.

4. The Pantheon, Rome: interior as depicted in a nineteenth-century engraving, showing the coffered interior of the dome and skylight oculus, originally the sole source of lighting. The interior is circular, with the diameter equaling the height of the dome, 43 m.

In contrast to the visible remains of the sacred areas of the city is the sense of the divine (*numen*) inspired by nature and the feeling of religious awe (*religio*), as described by Seneca the Younger (c. 4 BCE–65 CE).

> If you have ever come upon a grove that is thick with ancient trees rising far above their usual height and blocking the view of the sky with their cover of intertwining branches, the loftiness of the forest, the seclusion of the spot, and your wonder at the unbroken shade in the midst of open space will create in you a sense of the divine (*numen*). Or, if a cave made by the deep erosion of rocks supports a mountain with its arch, a place not made by hands but hollowed out by natural causes into spaciousness, then your mind will be aroused by a feeling of religious awe (*religio*). We venerate the sources of mighty rivers, we build an altar where a great stream suddenly bursts forth from a hidden source, we worship hot springs, and we deem lakes sacred because of their darkness or immeasurable depth. (Seneca the Younger, *Letters* 41.3)

The gods, however, could be benevolent or malevolent toward mankind; their existence and omnipresence were no guarantee of divine

5. View of Lake Nemi in the Alban Hills near Rome, from an original drawn by J. D. Harding and engraved by J. C. Vernall, c. 1830. Nemi was the site of an ancient shrine in a grove that was sacred to Diana, a goddess whose cult was adopted in Rome in the sixth century BCE.

goodwill. Characters in plays of Plautus (c. 254–184 BCE) comment upon the gods' capriciousness, remarks that surely reflect a commonly held view of their power. One Plautine character says that every outcome is in the hands of the gods (*Two Bacchises* 144). Another prays, "Jupiter, through whom we live the span of our lives, in whose control are all men's hopes of life, grant that this day may be free from harm" (*Little Carthaginian* 1187–1188).

In order to avert their anger, the gods' favor (*pax deorum*) had to be secured by regular prayer and sacrifice, the offering of an object that was of value to the donor. Cicero (106–43 BCE) defines *religio* as the *cultus deorum,* the worship of the gods (*On the Nature of the Gods* 2.8). The noun *cultus* is connected with the verb *colere,* which has a variety of meanings: to till, cultivate, tend, care for, honor, revere, and thus to worship. The assumption was that the gods would protect an individual or the state if their worship was properly maintained. Thus, traditional Roman religion was essentially pragmatic, a contractual relationship based on the so-called principle of *do ut des* (I give so that you *may* give). The gods were asked, and the hope was that they would respond favorably.

The gods' will was sought by divination, the observation and interpretation of signs believed to have been sent by the gods. In his treatise *On Divination* (1.3), Cicero notes that no public business was ever transacted at home or abroad without first taking the auspices – a term that originally meant the observation of the behavior of birds, but came to be more widely applied to a variety of signs thought to indicate divine favor or disfavor. One method of taking the auspices was by observing the feeding of caged chickens. If these sacred birds ate greedily when offered food, the gods were thought to favor the proposed business; otherwise, the business ought to be postponed.

Clearly divination was open to manipulation. Nonetheless, the several kinds of divination employed by the Romans, and its political importance, are reflected in Cicero's question "What people or state is not influenced by the pronouncements of interpreters of sacrificial entrails, prodigies [occurrences or phenomena that were strange or unusual and thus considered to have been sent by the gods], and lightning, those of augurs or astrologers, or of lots . . . , or the forewarning of dreams or of prophecy?" (*On Divination* 1.12).

For the Romans there was no clear distinction between religion and politics. State rituals were celebrated for the people at the state's expense by state officials (Festus 284 L). Many religious ceremonies, especially state festivals, were made conspicuous by the accompanying procession or parade, *pompa,* the Latin word from which our "pomp" derives. One of the most spectacular processions occurred at a military triumph, when the victorious general, dressed as the god Jupiter, entered the city accompanied by his soldiers, war captives, and a display of the booty he had seized. This victory parade made its way through the Forum Romanum to the temple of Jupiter on the Capitoline Hill.

Being a priest was not a full-time occupation, though most priest-hoods were held for life. Pontiffs and augurs, two of the most presti-gious male priesthoods, could and frequently did hold political office. For example, Julius Caesar (100–44 BCE) had been elected *pontifex maximus* (chief pontiff) before he held a major civic magistracy; only later did he have a distinguished political and military career. Many priests, as ex-magistrates, were members of the Senate, a body that was regularly consulted on religious matters. At a time when Rome governed an empire that extended throughout the Mediterranean world and was expanding northwards into Gaul, Cicero asked how anyone who acknowledged the existence of the gods could fail to realize that the Romans owed the creation, increase and, retention of their empire (*imperium*) to the will of the gods, as he declared, "We have excelled every race and nation in piety (*pietas*), in respect for religious matters (*religio*), and in that singular wisdom which recognizes that everything is ruled and controlled by the will of the gods" (*On the Reply of the Haruspices* 19).

A generation later, after Gaul and Egypt had been added to the Roman empire, the poet Virgil (70–19 BCE) asserted that Roman rule was god-given, having Jupiter declare, "I have given them [the Romans] empire without end" (*Aeneid* 1. 279).

6. "Maison Carrée" at Nîmes in France: a classic Roman temple with a high podium and steps leading up to the portico beyond which lies a walled chamber, the *cella*. This temple was originally dedicated to the goddess Roma and the emperor Augustus.

The altar, not the temple, was the focal point of the gods' worship. Altars were in the open and freestanding, though frequently located in front of a temple. On the altar, sacrifice was made to a particular deity in the hope or expectation that the favor would at some time be returned. The offering could be a simple bloodless sacrifice of fruit, flowers, cakes, honey, or wine, or a more costly blood sacrifice when one or more domestic animals would be killed.

Sacrifice and prayer for success were often accompanied by the vow to make another more enduring gift, if and when the petition was granted. The later offering could be modest or elaborate – a gold or silver bowl, a commemorative plaque, a statuette, a representation of the body part that had been healed, or spoils from a successful war. Such votive offerings were presented and usually kept in a temple or shrine to commemorate the donor's gratitude. A temple could itself be a votive offering, funded by a general from his victory spoils to com-memorate his success and express gratitude to the god for answering his prayer.

Cicero underscored the pragmatism of Roman religion when he asked, "Did anyone ever give thanks to the gods because he was a good man? No, he did so because he is rich, honored, and secure. Jupiter is called Best and Greatest not because he makes men just, moderate, and wise, but because he makes them healthy, secure, wealthy, and prosperous" (*On the Nature of the Gods* 3.87). When the Romans wanted to be informed about what was morally right, what was morally wrong, and what was neither one nor the other, they turned to philosophers, not to specialists in divination (Cicero, *On Divination* 2.10–11).

The Romans worshiped a wide range of gods. There were the greater anthropomorphized gods of Roman state religion such as Jupiter, Juno, and Mars; lesser divinities such as Castor, Hercules, and Flora (goddess of flowers); the Lar and Penates of the individual household; nonanthropomorphized divinities of the environment such as the spirits of streams, fountains, and woods; diseases affecting men, animals,

7. Third-century BCE coins depicting some of the earliest surviving representations of Roman deities: (a) Mars; (b) Minerva; (c) Jupiter, in a four-horse chariot driven by the winged goddess Victory; (d) Apollo; (e) Janus, the two-faced god.

and crops; abstractions such as Concord, Hope, and Mind; and also mortals who were deified after their death, for example, Julius Caesar, some emperors, and occasionally their wives.

Most of the greater anthropomorphized gods of Roman state religion resemble the Olympian gods of Greek mythology. Several deities were not originally Roman or even Italic, but had been assimilated or adopted from their neighbors, most notably the Greek colonists in southern Italy and Sicily, and the Etruscans to the north. Archaeology reveals the presence in the sixth century BCE of Greeks and Etruscans in the area of the Forum Boarium (Cattle Market) by the Tiber. The head of a terracotta statue of Minerva (Fig. 8) and a torso of Hercules, found near the church of S. Omobono, show the unmistakable characteristics of archaic Greek art of the late sixth century BCE. Well before the beginning of the fourth century BCE, Jupiter was assimilated with Zeus, Juno with Hera, Venus with Aphrodite, Diana with Artemis, Ceres with Demeter, Minerva with Athena, Mercury with Hermes, Vulcan with Hephaestus, Neptune with Poseidon, and Mars with Ares. But Janus, the god of beginnings who simultaneously faced in two directions,

8. Head of a statue of Minerva from the temple of Fortuna, found near S. Omobono in the Forum Boarium (Cattle Market), Rome.

is essentially Roman, while Vesta, the hearth goddess represented as a living flame, bears little resemblance to the Greek Hestia.

Assimilation does not imply a precise equivalence or identification. In the case of Mars, we should more correctly speak of syncretism, since the original Italic deity seems to have been connected more with agriculture than war. The two Greek deities Apollo and Dionysus (also known as Bacchus), retained their Greek names, though the latter was also identified with the Roman deity Liber. The vow to build a temple to Apollo in 433 BCE for the people's health at a time of plague indicates that Apollo's original cult in Rome was that of healer (Livy 4.25), not the more familiar god of prophecy worshiped at Delphi in Greece.

Moreover, the major deities of Rome often bore cult titles or epithets not found in Greek mythology and literature. For example, Jupiter Best and Greatest (*Optimus Maximus*) was worshiped on the Capitoline Hill, sharing an Etruscan-style temple with Juno and Minerva.

9. Model of the triple temple of Jupiter Best and Greatest, Juno, and Minerva on the Capitoline Hill. In contrast to later Roman temples (see Fig. 6), Etruscan temples were squat and square rather than rectangular. The superstructure was of wood and brick or stone, and the roof was decorated with painted terracotta tiles, often with statuary along the ridgepole.

In this temple were kept the Sibylline Books, a collection of prophecies said to have been bought from the Sibyl of Cumae by the Etruscan king Tarquin the Elder (616–579 BCE) who, with his son Tarquin the Proud (534–510 BCE), was responsible for the construction of this magnificent temple. Jupiter was also worshiped in two other temples in Rome, as Thunderer and as Stayer in Battle. Juno was worshiped as Queen (Regina) on the Aventine Hill, and she had another temple as Protectress (Sospita) in the Forum Holitorium, a cult that probably originated in Lanuvium, some twenty miles south of Rome.

10. Statue of Juno Sospita (Protectress) from Lanuvium, wearing a goatskin, holding a shield, and brandishing a spear as she advances to battle. The goatskin and stance as a warrior goddess are attributes of the Greek goddess Athena, rather than of Hera (who is generally associated with Juno).

In contrast to the state rituals celebrated in public areas, private rituals were enacted at simple altars and shrines. The poet Horace (65–8 BCE) describes a blood sacrifice that he will make to a country spring near his birthplace at the Fontinalia, a festival honoring the god of springs and fountains.

> O spring of Bandusia, more shining than glass, worthy of sweet wine and flowers, tomorrow you will be honored with the gift of a young kid. His brow, just swelling with budding horns, marks him out for love and battles. But in vain. This offspring of the lively flock will stain your cool waters with its own red blood. (Horace, *Odes* 3.13.1–8)

Family rituals usually were celebrated by the head of the household (*paterfamilias*) for members of the immediate family (*gens*) and the extended family or household (*familia*) that included slaves and their families. In the prologue to his play *Pot of Gold,* Plautus has the Lar, the protecting deity of the house, address the audience in a speech that

11. Four bronze statuettes of household, or family, Lares. Such statuettes were a feature of Roman houses. Each Lar holds a *rhyton* (drinking horn) and a *patera* (libation bowl).

articulates the contractual nature of the *do ut des* concept and the need for the family to keep its own particular gods placated:

> So that no one may wonder who I am, I'll briefly introduce myself. I am the Lar of the family of this home that you saw me come from. For many years now I have been in possession of this house. I looked after it for the father and grandfather of the present occupant. As a suppliant, the grandfather secretly entrusted to me a pot of gold. He buried it in the center of the hearth, entreating me to guard it for him. . . .
>
> After the death of the man who entrusted the gold to me, I began to observe whether his son would pay me greater honor than his father. But his devotion to me soon diminished, and I had a smaller and smaller share of honor. So I did the same by him, and he died. He left a son who now occupies this house, a man of the same sort as his father and grandfather. He has one daughter. She is constantly praying to me every day, with gifts of incense or wine or something. She gives me garlands. Because of her devotion, I have caused her father Euclio to discover the treasure here so that he might more easily find her a husband, if he is willing. (Plautus, *Pot of Gold* 1–27)

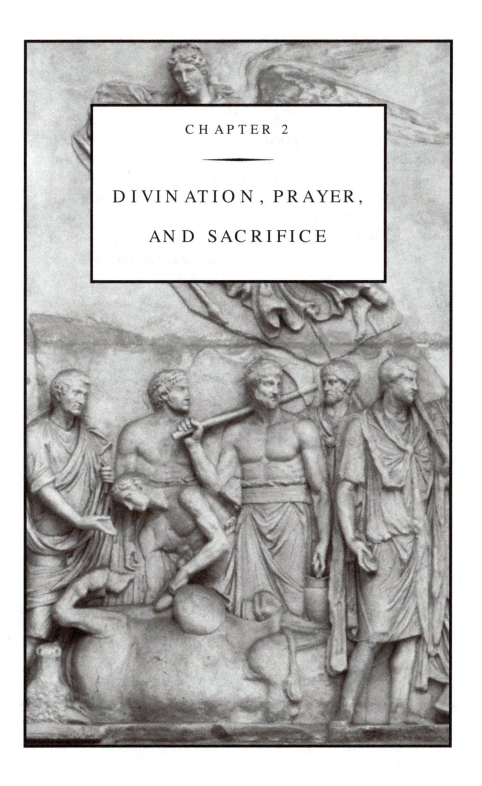

CHAPTER 2

DIVINATION, PRAYER,
AND SACRIFICE

The whole religious practice (*religio*) of the Roman people is divided into ritual (*sacra*), auspices (*auspicia*), and prophetic warnings. . . . I have always thought that none of these areas of religion are to be despised, since I am convinced that Romulus by his auspices and Numa by his establishment of ritual laid the foundations of our state, which assuredly could never have been as great as it is had we not maintained the fullest measure of divine favor. (Cicero, *On the Nature of the Gods* 3.5)

More than one kind of divination is used in public and in private. To say nothing of other peoples, how many kinds have our own people embraced! Initially, according to tradition, Romulus, the father of this city, not only founded it with due auspices, but he himself was an excellent augur. Then other kings used other augurs and, after the expulsion of the kings, no public business was ever transacted at home or abroad without first taking the auspices. (Cicero, *On Divination* 1.3)

As these excerpts from Cicero indicate, tradition retrojected Rome's religious institutions back to her mythical past, attributing the institution of the auspices and divination to Rome's founder, Romulus, and the establishment of ritual to Numa, Romulus' successor as king. The poet Ovid (43 BCE–17 CE) tells how Romulus and his brother Remus took the auspices to decide which of them should be the founder of Rome.

The question was: which of the two should be the founder. "There is no need of a contest," said Romulus, "great faith is put in birds. Let us try the bird omen." This was approved. In the morning one went to the rocks of the wooded Palatine, the other approached the top of the Aventine. Remus saw six birds, Romulus twice that number, one after another. They stood by their agreement and Romulus took control of the city. (Ovid, *Fasti* 4.812–818)

The historian Livy (64 or 59 BCE–17 CE) relates the story of how Numa instilled the fear of the gods in his people by fabricating a miraculous story in which he pretended to have nightly meetings with the goddess Egeria. "On her advice," said Numa, "I am instituting the religious rituals (*sacra*) that were most approved by the gods." Among other religious institutions attributed to Numa are the appointment of special priests, including the pontiffs and Vestal Virgins, the building of a temple to Janus, and the introduction of a twelve-month calendar (Livy 1.19–20). When and how these religious institutions actually developed, however, is impossible to discern.

Among the different kinds of divination are the interpretation of the entrails of sacrificial victims, prodigies, lightning, augury, astrology, lots, dreams, and prophecies (Cicero, *On Divination* 1.12). The presence in Rome in the late third and second centuries BCE of religious hucksters offering a variety of services to the general populace is attested by derogatory references in Plautus and Ennius (239–169 BCE). In Plautus' *Braggart Soldier* 692–694, a bachelor lists the various female hucksters who prey on superstitious women and would have to be paid each month were he to take a wife. Included are the woman who utters incantations, the dream interpreter, the clairvoyant, the woman who divines from entrails, and the one who observes the sky. Ennius gives his opinion of such charlatans:

I think nothing of Marsian augurs, local entrail diviners, astrologers who hang around the circus, Isis seers, or interpreters of dreams. They are not diviners either by knowledge or skill. Rather they are superstitious seers, shameless prophets, who are lazy, mad, or ruled by want. They do not know what path to take for themselves, yet they show the way to others. They beg a coin from those to whom they promise riches. Let them deduct their fee from what they promise and give back the rest. (Ennius, as quoted in Cicero, *On Divination* 1.132)

Since no public business was conducted without first taking the auspices (Cicero, *On Divination* 1.3), it is not surprising that most of the extant information about the rituals of divination, prayer, and sacrifice is found in a political or military context. Most prayers are petitionary, including vows, oaths, and prayers of supplication or propitiation. Other kinds of prayer are those of thanksgiving, expiation, dedication, lamentation, adoration, and confession, of which examples of the last three are rare in the surviving sources. In any kind of prayer, precautions had to be taken to ensure that no error (*vitium*) might prevent its fulfillment. Formulaic invocations were like passwords that opened communication with the gods. If any mistake in the prayers or the ritual should occur, the gods would not respond to the request.

Pliny the Elder (23/24–79 CE) noted that prayer was an essential component of sacrifice or any form of divination, while also emphasizing the need for accuracy, precision, and music to exclude extraneous noise.

Sacrificing victims or consulting the gods without also making a prayer apparently does no good. Some words are appropriate for seeking favorable omens, others for averting evil, yet others for praise.

We see that our highest magistrates appeal to the gods with set prayers. In order that no word be omitted or spoken out of place, one attendant dictates the prayer in advance from a script, another is assigned to keep a close check on it, and a third is appointed to enforce silence. In addition, a flutist plays so that nothing but the prayer is heard. Remarkable cases of

12. Panel from the triumphal arch of Marcus Aurelius, Rome, 176 CE. This sculptured relief depicts the sacrifice at the conclusion of Marcus Aurelius' triumph. The emperor, his head covered, is offering a libation at a small altar in front of the temple of Jupiter on the Capitol. A young male attendant (*camillus*) holds an incense box, and a musician plays to exclude extraneous sounds. At far right is a bare-chested slave who handles and eventually kills the victim.

two kinds are recorded, where either ill-omened noises have ruined the ritual or an error has been made in the prayer itself. (Pliny the Elder, *Natural History* 28.11)

The instructions given by Cato the Elder (234–149 BCE) for purifying a farm by means of the sacrifice of a pig, sheep, and bull include formulaic prayers as an integral part of the ritual in which the victims were led in procession around the farmstead before being killed. The prayers – precise and repetitious to ensure their efficacy – requested the welfare of the owner's house (his immediate family, *domus*) and his household (extended family, *familia*, that would have included the slaves). In addition to Jupiter, the deities invoked are Janus as god of beginnings and Mars as god of agriculture.

Invoke Janus and Jupiter with an offering of wine. Then speak these words: Father Mars, I pray and beseech you to be benevolent and well-disposed toward me, my house, and my household. With this intent I have ordered a pig-sheep-bull procession to be led around my field, land, and farm, so that you will keep away, ward off, and avert diseases, both seen

13. Sacrifice of a pig, sheep, and bull (*suovetaurilia*), depicted on a Tiberian relief in the Louvre. (Ryberg 1955: 106–109)

14. Bronze figurine of a Roman worshiper, his head veiled, as he holds an incense box.

and unseen, barrenness, crop losses, disasters, and unseasonable weather; so that you will allow the harvests, the grain crops, the vineyards, and the orchards to flourish and achieve a productive maturity; so that you will protect the shepherds and the flocks, and bestow good health and strength upon me, my house, and my household. (Cato, *On Agriculture* 141)

The Romans usually sacrificed with the head covered. In the case of Apollo and Ceres, however, sacrifice was made in the Greek mode, with the head uncovered, apparently because these deities were considered to retain something of their Greek origin. Bloodless sacrifice was the more common practice, animal sacrifice being reserved for special occasions. Blood sacrifice victims were usually domestic animals: pigs, sheep, goats, cattle, or occasionally dogs. The victims chosen for sacrifice had to be without physical blemish, and a distinction was made between full-grown and younger animals.

In a public blood sacrifice, animal victims were led in a procession (*pompa*) by slave attendants to an altar situated in front of a temple of

15. Small frieze from inside the Altar of Augustan Peace (*Ara Pacis Augustae*), Rome, depicting a procession with priests, animals, and the bare-chested slave attendants handling the animals.

the deity to whom sacrifice was being made. The priests or officiants would wash their hands with water from a special vessel. Silence was ordered with the ritual cry "Check your tongues." The main officiant, his toga pulled over his head like a veil, would say a prayer, offering wine and perhaps incense as a libation on the altar. The animal's head was held by a young male attendant (*camillus*), as a few hairs were plucked and placed on the altar. Meal (flour mingled with salt) was mixed with wine and poured over the victim's head. The slave attendants would perform the actual slaughter, with the officiant looking on.

16. Panel from the altar of Scipio Orfitus (295 CE) depicting the sacrificant, his head veiled, as he pours wine and meal over the animal's head. A young male attendant (*camillus*) holds the victim, a steer.

Foreigners, prisoners in chains, women, and girls were excluded from participation in the essential moments of state sacrificial ritual (Festus 72 L).

The poet Lucretius (c. 94–55 or 51 BCE) describes the practice of blood sacrifice, which he unequivocally deplores: "Piety does not mean appearing regularly with covered head, turning to a stone, approaching every altar, falling prostrate on the ground with palms outstretched before the gods' shrines, showering the altars with the blood of beasts, and heaping vow upon vow" (*On the Nature of Things* 5.1198–1202). The killing would literally have been a bloody business, requiring considerable skill and brute force on the part of the slave attendants who, for practical reasons, were naked above the waist. Truly awesome would have been the stench of blood, guts, and excrement, which could hardly have been disguised by incense.

A blow to the head would cause the victim to fall to its knees, its throat was cut, and the carcass opened up. *Haruspices,* priests who specialized in divination, would then examine the entrails to see whether the sacrifice was acceptable to the gods. If any imperfection (*vitium*) was discovered, the ceremony had to be started anew and another victim sacrificed in order to avert the gods' anger. Once the sacrifice was approved, parts of the approved victim were burned on the altar as an

17. Silver cup from Boscoreale (early first century CE), depicting a slave with an ax poised ready to strike the victim. In the background is a representation of the temple of Jupiter on the Capitoline.

18. Part of a relief (from a restored cast) from Trajan's Forum in Rome (mid-second century CE) shows a *haruspex* examining a victim's entrails; in the background are two slave attendants, one with an ax. (Ryberg 1955: 128–130)

offering to the god. The participants would then feast on the remaining meat. For poorer citizens, the sacrifice of a large number of animals at a major public festival would have afforded a rare opportunity to eat meat.

Plautus offers a clever parody of a sacrifice in which a pimp is trying to win the favor of Venus, goddess of love. After six victims have proved unacceptable, the pimp gives up and boasts that, because the gods are apparently angry with him, he himself has grown so angry that he refuses to give Venus her share of the meat.

> May the gods, one and all, damn the pimp who after this day sacrifices a single victim to Venus, or offers her a single grain of incense. Here I am, damned in the eyes of my gods who are angry at me. Six times today I've sacrificed a lamb, yet not one sign of favor could I get from Venus. And so, seeing I can't get good omens, I've gone off in anger myself, forbidding anyone to cut off the god's share of the meat. That's the neat way I've caught her out, that greedy Venus. She wasn't willing to let enough be enough – so I called a halt myself. That's the way I take action. (Plautus, *Little Carthaginian* 449–459)

On a more serious note, prayers of supplication or propitiation were made in times of crisis. During the Second Punic War (218–201

BCE), when Hannibal, the Carthaginian general, had invaded Italy, women played a prominent role in a two-day ceremony of public supplication held after reports of several prodigies, including a lightning strike on the temple of Juno the Queen. *Haruspices* advised that the goddess must be appeased by a gift. The matrons offered a golden bowl. On the second day, a special hymn composed by one of the leading poets was sung by a procession of twenty-seven maidens as they made their way to Juno's temple.

> From the temple of Apollo two white cows were led through the Porta Carmentalis into the city. Behind them were carried two cypress-wood statues of Juno the Queen. Then came twenty-seven maidens, clad in long robes, singing the hymn in honor of Juno the Queen.... Behind the line of maidens there followed the decemvirs [priests in charge of sacrifices], wearing laurel crowns and purple-bordered togas.... In the Forum the procession halted, and the maidens advanced, passing a rope from hand to hand and tempering the sound of their voices to the beat of their steps. Then they proceeded...to the temple of Juno the Queen. There the two victims were sacrificed by the decemvirs, and the cypress-wood statues carried into the temple. (Livy 27.37)

Before a military undertaking, the commander would vow, or promise, to return the favor of the gods should his request be granted and the mission prove successful. A temple to Bellona, goddess of war, was vowed at a crucial moment in a battle against two long-standing foes, the Etruscans and Samnites (296 BCE). Livy (10.19) describes how the commander lifted his hands to the sky, praying, "Bellona, if today you grant victory to us, then I vow you a temple." Later a temple was built and dedicated on the Campus Martius, funded by part of the victory spoils.

The piety of otherwise unknown individuals is memorialized by more modest votive offerings and inscriptions commemorating the

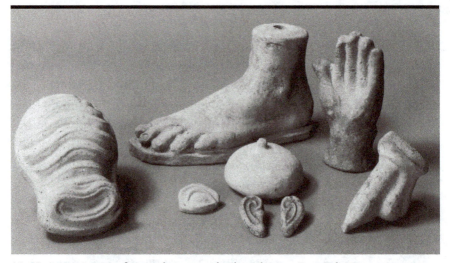

19. Votive terracottas from a shrine to a healing deity at Ponte di Nona, some nine miles east of Rome. These models of various body parts reflect the curative powers of this sanctuary. Third or second century BCE.

fulfillment of vows. An inscribed plaque was dedicated to Minerva the Mindful by a woman named Tullia Superiana in gratitude for the restoration of her hair (*CIL* 11.1305; *ILS* 3135). An inscription found on the road to Ostia commemorates the sacrifice of a white cow made in fulfillment of a vow by a slave for the recovery of his sight.

> Felix Asianus, public slave of the pontiffs, gladly and sincerely discharged his vow of a white heifer to rustic Bona Dea Felicula [Good Goddess Felicula] for the restoration of his eyesight. He had been given up by the doctors, but after ten months he was cured by the favor of the Mistress and her remedies. (*CIL* 6.68)

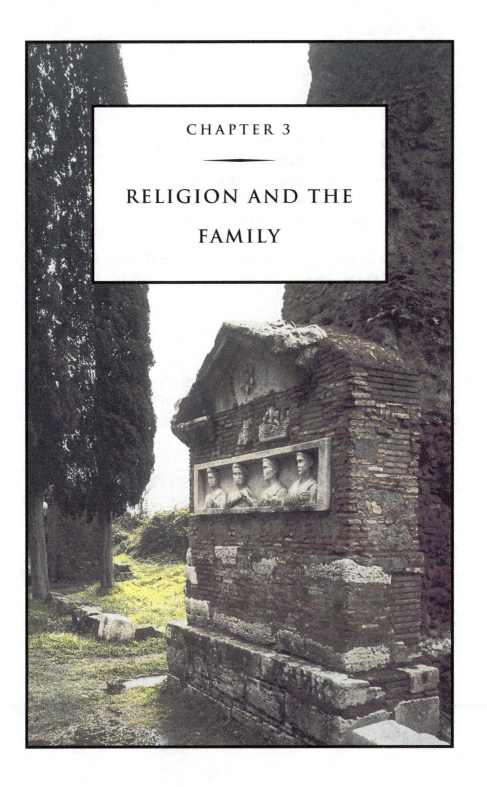

# CHAPTER 3

## RELIGION AND THE FAMILY

Privately they shall worship those gods that they have duly received from their ancestors. In cities they shall have shrines; in the country they shall have groves and places for the Lares. They shall preserve the rites of their family (*familia*) and their ancestors (*patres*). (Cicero, *On the Laws* 2.19)

The sacred rites of individuals (*sacra privata*) shall endure for ever. (Cicero, *On the Laws* 2.22)

---

In a Roman context, "family" extends beyond our usual concepts of nuclear and extended family to include household slaves and their offspring. The laws of the Twelve Tables deriving from the mid-fifth century BCE reveal the extent of *patria potestas,* the power of the *paterfamilias* (father of the family) who had the power of life or death over the entire household. As is apparent in the prologue to Plautus' *Pot of Gold,* it was the duty of the *paterfamilias* to tend the family cult, maintain the *pax deorum,* and so ensure the well-being of the whole household. Cato's prayer of purification for his farm (*On Agriculture* 141) included the welfare of his crops and trees, the protection and welfare of his shepherds and their flocks, and good health and strength for himself, his family (*domus*), and his household (*familia*). Also included in the duties of the *paterfamilias* was the conducting of rituals concerned with birth, marriage, and death. Because these rituals were performed within the family and were not a matter of public record, the surviving literary evidence is scanty.

Each Roman home had its own protective deities: the Lar (plural, Lares), protecting the household or family; the Penates, protecting the stores-cupboard or pantry (*penus*) in the inner part of the house; the

20. Household shrine from the House of Vettii in Pompeii. In the tympanum (a) are the symbols of sacrifice: a *patera* at the center, with a knife on the right and animal's skull on the left. Painted figures of Lares (b) holding drinking horns and wine buckets flank (c) the Genius of the family who is holding an incense box in his left hand. (d) A serpent moves toward offerings on a small altar. The serpent, a common motif of these shrines, probably represents fertility, and thus the prosperity of the household.

Genius or guardian spirit of individual members of the household, especially the *paterfamilias;* and Vesta, goddess of the hearth. The shrine to the Lar, generally known as the *lararium,* was sometimes in the *atrium,* the more public part of the house near the entrance, but more commonly in the kitchen area. Just as the home had its tutelary deities, so too did the entire property. The poet Martial (c. 40–104 CE) lists the tutelary deities of the different areas of his farm, which include Jupiter the Thunderer, Silvanus (a woodland deity), Diana, Mars, and Flora, the goddess of flowering or blossoming plants (Martial, *Epigrams* 10.92).

Although the general picture is one of male predominance, women also made offerings to the gods on their own behalf. In Plautus' *Pot of Gold* (23–25), the daughter of the house makes an offering at the family shrine. In *Merchant* (678–680), a woman places a laurel branch on an altar, praying to Apollo for the well-being of her son: "Apollo, I pray that in your benevolence you bestow favor (*pax*), good health, and good sense on our household (*familia*). In your benevolence may you also spare my son." In public supplications, however, women generally played subordinate roles, as we saw in Chapter 2 in the procession of twenty-seven maidens singing a hymn (Livy 27.37).

Upon marriage, a woman would pass from her father's control to the *manus* (hand) of her husband, thus losing her place in her natal family to join that of her husband. But in later times, especially among the nobility and the more affluent, marriage without *manus* became

21. Relief from the Altar of Augustan Peace (Ara Pacis, Rome) showing the family of the emperor Augustus with their children in a ceremonial procession.

22. Marriage scene on an ancient sarcophagus (late third or fourth century CE), now in S. Lorenzo fuori le Mura, Rome. On the right is depicted the joining of hands (*iunctio dextrarum*) of the bride and bridegroom. At the center a crouching attendant holds the victim, a sheep. The left half is occupied by allegorical figures. The tablet (top center) would originally have shown the burial inscription. (Ryberg 1955: 166–167)

more common. A marriage would be arranged with the parents of the groom by the bride's father or her guardian, or by the groom himself in the case of an older man or one who was already a *paterfamilias*. The importance of dowry is apparent in Plautus' *Pot of Gold,* where the Lar says that he will repay the daughter's offerings by causing her father to discover the buried pot of gold "so that he might more easily find her a husband" (*Pot of Gold* 25–27). The purpose of marriage was the procreation of legitimate children to ensure the continuation of the family. Livy has Romulus express the ideals of Roman marriage in his effort to placate the Sabine women after their forcible abduction: "You will be in marriage and will enjoy partnership of all our fortunes, of citizenship, and of children, the dearest thing that there is for human beings" (Livy 1.9).

The general details of an upper-class Roman wedding are apparent from a variety of literary sources and iconographic evidence. A reference by Cicero indicates that auspices were taken (*On Divination* 1.28). Friends and clients of both families would assemble at the house of the bride's father or guardian, probably in the *atrium,* an open area in the front part of the house. The bride would be ritually dressed for her wedding, her hair arranged in six locks with woolen ribbons. She would wear a white woven tunic fastened at the waist and a flame-colored veil with shoes of the same color. On the bridegroom's arrival, the words of consent would be spoken and the matron of honor would join the right hands of the bride and bridegroom. A sacrifice would be made, usually a pig or a sheep. After the signing of the marriage contract, there was a wedding feast. The bride was then taken in a procession to her new home, where the bridegroom received and carried her over the threshold to avoid the ill omen of a stumble. In the *atrium* of her new home, she would receive fire and water from her husband, symbolizing her authority within her new home. She would offer a coin to both the Lar of the family and to the Lares Compitales, the guardian deities of her new neighborhood. She would then be led into the bedchamber, where she was attended by married women. Then, as a wedding song was sung, the bridegroom was admitted.

To celebrate the birth of a child, a fire was kindled on the hearth and kept burning for several days after the birth; male children were named on the ninth day from birth and female children on the eight (Plutarch, *Roman Questions* 102; Macrobius, *Sat* 1.16, 36; Festus 107 L). On assuming the toga of manhood (*toga virilis*), a youth would dedicate his *bulla,* an amulet worn by male children as a protection from harm, at the shrine of the Lares (Persius, *Satires* 5.30–31). Here too, on the day before her marriage, a girl would dedicate her dolls and toys (Varro, in Nonius 863. 15 L).

In the *atria* of the nobility were painted wax likenesses of family ancestors. According to Pliny the Elder, these were "faces rendered in wax that were set out in separate cupboards, so that there were like-nesses (*imagines*) to accompany family funerals" (*Natural History* 35.6). The Greek historian Polybius (c. 200–c. 118 BCE) remarks that "the likeness was a mask (*prosopon*) that reproduced with remarkable fidelity both the features and complexion of the deceased." These masks were worn in the funeral procession by the family members who most resembled a deceased ancestor (Polybius 6.53).

23 (*above*). Household shrine with busts of family ancestors, in exedra 25 in the House of Menander, Pompeii.

24 (*right*). Statue from Ostia, near Rome, of a man with busts of his ancestors.

According to the laws of the Twelve Tables, it was forbidden to bury or burn a dead person within the city. Tombs of the rich and famous lined the sides of the great roads leading out of Rome and most major cities throughout the Roman Empire, corroborating the remark of the nouveau riche freedman Trimalchio, "It's quite mistaken to have elaborate houses to live in while you are alive, and not be concerned about the houses that we must inhabit for a longer time" (Petronius, *Satyricon* 71). The affluent would have had no problem in funding an elaborate and expensive tomb, but people of lesser means had to rely on wealthy patrons to grant them space in their family memorial or, in the case of those who had no patron, on *collegia* (associations or clubs) formed to ensure a funeral for their members.

An inscription from the early second century CE preserves the rules of a *collegium* at Lanuvium, south of Rome. There was an entry fee, and monthly dues were required. If dues were not paid for six consecutive months, a funeral would not be provided. The club granted a fixed amount for the funeral of a paid-up member, with a fee for participants

25 (*above*). Relief from Amiternum in central Italy, depicting the funerary procession of a member of the local elite. The deceased is represented propped up on a bier that is being carried in a procession, with musicians playing various instruments. The women of the family are shown in the upper-left register.

26 (*left*). Via Appia Antica outside Rome, where the remains of Roman tombs still line the road.

27 (*below*). Funerary relief of Gaius Marullus and his family.

28. Tomb of Pomponius Hylas (first century CE) on the Via Appia Antica. In this kind of tomb, known as a columbarium (literally "dovecote"), an urn containing the ashes of the deceased was placed in one of the niches, sometimes along with a bust. The ashes of slaves, freedmen, and freedwomen were often deposited in a family columbarium.

in the funeral procession. To avoid the expense of hiring vehicles, the mourners were to walk. If a member died in a location more than twenty miles from Lanuvium, three men were chosen to arrange the funeral, and they had to account for their expenses. Club members met regularly for dinners, under rules to prevent unacceptable behavior (*CIL* 14.2112th = *ILS* 7212). Such associations thus served a social purpose for the less affluent while also guaranteeing a decent funeral. Those who were too poor to belong to such a club were buried anonymously in a mass grave or cremated in a public crematorium. Martial writes of a group of corpse bearers carrying a pauper's body "like the thousand that the wretched pyre receives" (*Epigrams* 8.75.9–10).

After noting that family rituals (*sacra privata*) shall endure for ever, Cicero makes three stipulations: "The rights (*iura*) of the *manes* (spirits or shades of the dead) shall be sacred. Consider dead kinsfolk as gods; the expenditure and mourning for them shall be limited" (*On the Laws* 2.22). Ovid describes the rituals at the Parentalia and Feralia, festivals of the dead that were celebrated from 18 to 21 February:

> The tombs also are honored. Appease the spirits (*animae*) of your fathers and bring small gifts to the extinguished funeral pyres. The shades (*manes*) ask but little: rather than an expensive

gift, piety (*pietas*) is what is welcome. The gods that inhabit the depths of the Styx [a river in the Underworld] are not greedy. A tile covered with a wreath of garlands, a sprinkling of grain, a small pinch of salt, bread soaked in wine, and some loose violets, these are enough. Put these in a potsherd and leave it in the middle of the road. I do not forbid larger offerings, though a shade (*umbra*) is appeased even by these. Add prayers and the appropriate words at the hearths that have been set up. (Ovid, *Fasti* 2.533–542)

Inscriptions and epitaphs carved on tombs or grave markers are an important source of information about people who otherwise would

29. House-tombs at Isola Sacra, near Ostia. These tombs were intended for multiple burials, both cremation and inhumation. Note the masonry couches for ritual meals honoring the dead. The inscription on the tomb in the center reads: "To the spirits of the departed. Quintus Appius Saturninus, son of Quintus, built this for himself and for Annia Donata, his well-deserving wife, and for their children and ex-slaves, male and female, and for their descendants" (BNP 2.104–105).

30. Isola Sacra: interior of a house-tomb with small niches for cremation urns. Under the large niche on the right is an inscription commemorating a woman, Varia Servanda: "To the spirits of the departed. Ampelus and Ennychis erected this with their own money for Vaia Servanda, the daughter of Publius" (BNP 2.106).

be unknown to history. These inscriptions are often addressed to the passerby, offering a message from the dead to the living, while also giving a brief biographical note that expresses family values and occasionally refers to an afterlife. Many of these monuments memorialize freedpersons who identify themselves by their profession. The inscription on the funerary relief of a freedman butcher and his wife, Lucius Aurelius Hermia and Aurelia Philematium, commemorates conjugal ideals of chastity and affection.

> Lucius Aurelius Hermia, freedman of Lucius, a butcher on the Viminal Hill. She who preceded me in death was my one and only wife; chaste in body, with a loving spirit, she lived faithful to her faithful husband, with an affection equal to mine. Utterly selfless, she never shirked her duties.

31. Funerary relief of Lucius Aurelius Hermia and his wife, Aurelia Philematium, from Rome, c. 75–50 BCE.

While I lived, I was called Aurelia Philematium, a woman chaste and modest, unknown to the common crowd, faithful to her husband. My husband, whom, alas, I have now left, was a fellow freedman. He was truly like a father to me. When I was seven years old he cared for me. Now I am forty and in the power of death. My husband flourished through my constant care. (*CIL* 6.9499; *ILS* 7472)

The epitaph of Veturia, wife of a Roman legionary serving in the province of Pannonia (in the Danube area), is a reminder of the short life expectancy that would have been the lot of most in the Greco-Roman world.

Here I lie, a married woman named Veturia. My father was Veturius, my husband Fortunatus. I lived for twenty-seven years, and I was married for sixteen years to the same man. After I gave birth to six children, only one of whom is still alive, I died. Titus Fortunatus, a soldier of Legion II Adiutrix, provided this memorial for his wife who was incomparable and showed outstanding devotion (*pietas*) to him. (*CIL* 3.3572)

32. The lower part of the funerary stele of Publius Longidienus, who is shown working as a shipbuilder. A small tablet above the right half of the ship records that he is busy with his job (*ad onus properat*). The two busts above this scene depict and name two freedmen of Publius Longidienus, Rufio and Pilades. In the upper part of the stele (not shown here) are busts of Publius Longidienus, who is stated to have been a shipwright (*faber navalis*), and his wife. (*CIL* XI 139)

Two inscriptions from Rome memorialize prematurely deceased adult males.

Mercurius lived twenty-five years, six months, twenty days, and four hours. His very loving brother and his mistress Julia provided this memorial for one who was well-deserving. (*CIL* 6.22417)

Publius Malius Firminus lived twenty-four years, three months, and twenty-seven days. Publius Malius Maximus provided this memorial for his well-deserving brother. (*CIL* 6.21874)

Despite some references to an afterlife, the more common view – that there is nothing after death – is reflected in the following epitaph on a third-century CE tomb with a representation of the deceased reclining at a banquet or feast.

Tibur was my home; Flavius Agricola my name. I am the one you see reclining there, just as I used to do among the living at dinner, carefully looking after myself for all the years that Fate granted me. Nor was I ever sparing with the wine. My beloved wife, Flavia Primitiva, died before me, a chaste and attentive worshiper of Isis. With her I spent thirty years of happiness. For consolation, she left me her offspring – Aurelius Primitivus, who will tend our grave with piety and preserve our resting place forever. Friends who read this, pay attention to what I say: mix the wine, bind the festive garland around your brow, drink far from here [the tomb]. And do not refrain from the pleasures of love with beautiful women. When death comes, everything will be consumed by earth and fire. (*CIL* 6.17985a)

Numerous tombstones express the finality of death by the letters "nf f ns nc" (*non fui, fui, non sum, non curo* – I didn't exist, I did exist, I don't exist, I have no cares). A hopeful view is expressed by an epitaph-prayer from Rome lamenting the premature death of a seven-year-old girl:

O serene peace of the inhabitants of the underworld and you renowned spirits of the pious who dwell in the sacred areas of Erebus, conduct innocent Magnilla through the groves and the Elysian fields directly to your resting places. She was snatched away in her eighth year by the harsh fates while she was enjoying the time of tender youth. She was beautiful and sensitive, clever beyond her years, lovely, sweet, and charming. This unfortunate child who was so quickly deprived of her life must be mourned with perpetual lament and tears. (*CIL* 6.21846)

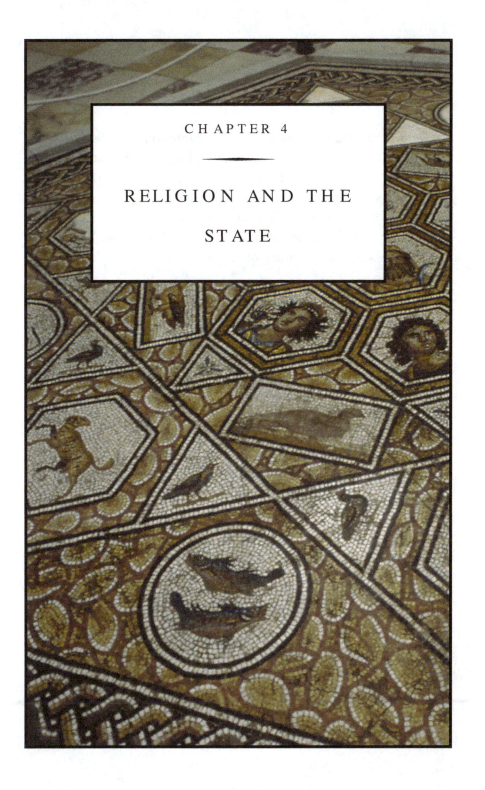

CHAPTER 4

RELIGION AND THE

STATE

Among the many divinely inspired institutions established by our ancestors, nothing is more outstanding than their desire to have the same individuals in control over worship of the gods and the vital interests of the state. Their objective was to ensure that the most eminent and illustrious citizens maintain religion by their good government of the state, and maintain the state by their wise interpretation of religion. (Cicero, *On His House* 1.1)

No public business was ever transacted at home or abroad without first taking the auspices. (Cicero, *On Divination* 1.3)

---

In public life, the rituals of prayer and sacrifice were led by official priests acting on behalf of the state. Most priests of state religion were male and held office for life, one notable exception being the Vestal Virgins, the priestesses of Vesta. Vestals served full-time, whereas male priests were engaged only part-time in their priestly duties and frequently had active political and military careers. A man who had held a major political office automatically became a member of the Senate, a body that was consulted on both political and religious matters. Thus Cicero (*On His House* 1.1) notes the wisdom of having the same men controlling the worship of the gods and the vital interests of the state. The tradition of taking the auspices further exemplifies the inextricable relationship between religion and politics: the gods' will had to be sought before any public business was initiated, be it political or military.

Originally, members of only a few families, the patricians, were eligible for a priesthood and entitled to take the auspices. After plebeians were admitted to priesthoods in 300 BCE, the only official requirements for selection were Roman citizenship, free birth, and the absence of physical defects. Generally priests were not attached to a deity or temple, but rather were assigned particular duties: augurs dealt with questions of augural law and the taking of auspices; fetial priests attended to the making of treaties and declaration of war. Exceptions were the *flamen Dialis* (priest of Jupiter), the *flamen Martialis* (priest of Mars), the *flamen* of Quirinus (a deity assimilated with the deified Romulus), and the Vestal Virgins.

The rules imposed on the *flamen Dialis* virtually denied the incumbent the possibility of pursuing a political or military career. He was not allowed to ride a horse or see an army equipped for battle, nor was he permitted to take an oath, handle flames, or wear clothing that involved a knot. In the open air he always had to wear a special cap, the

33. Relief from the Altar of Augustan Peace (Ara Pacis), Rome, depicting a procession of the imperial family with (*left*) two priests, *flamines,* each wearing a cloak-like garment, not a toga, and a distinctive headdress, a woolen cap or bonnet (*apex*) with a spike on the crown. They are followed by two sacrificants, their heads covered, one of whom bears an ax, and by members of the imperial family, including a child.

*apex*. He had to sleep in a special bed from which he was not allowed to be absent for three nights in succession. If his wife died, he had to resign his priesthood. He could not enter a place where there was a tomb or touch a dead body, although he was not prohibited from attending a funeral (Gellius, *Attic Nights* 10.15.1–25). Such taboos suggest the antiquity of this priesthood.

34 (*left*). Marble relief depicting the Temple of Vesta in the Roman Forum (early empire).

35 (*below*). Roman Forum with the Palatine in the background. (*Left*) three columns of the temple of Vesta; (*center*) three larger columns of the temple of Castor.

The cult of Vesta was also of great antiquity. The Vestal Virgins played a vital role in state religion by tending the sacred flame that represented the goddess and by preparing meal (flour mixed with salt) for all public sacrifices. The extinction of this flame would portend destruction of the city. The Vestals lived in the goddess' sanctuary in the Forum and were required to remain unmarried and chaste for thirty years, offering sacrifices and performing other rites ordained by law. The first ten years were spent learning these rites; the second ten performing them; and the third ten teaching them to others. After thirty years, they were free to depart and marry, but most remained virgins in the goddess' sanctuary until their deaths, when another was chosen by the pontiffs to fill the vacancy. A girl between six and ten years old, both of whose parents were still living, would be "taken" from her father's home by the *pontifex maximus* (chief pontiff), as if she were a captive taken in war. She was escorted to the House of the Vestals and handed over to the pontiffs, thus passing from the control of her father without the ceremony of emancipation or loss of her civil rights. She did, however, acquire the right to make a will (Gellius, *Attic Nights* 1.12.1–14).

36. Remains of the Atrium Vestae, the residence of the Vestals located between the temple of Vesta and the Domus Publica (State House), with statues of Vestals.

Offenses committed by Vestals were examined and punished by the pontiffs. For lesser offenses a Vestal was whipped, but those who lost their virginity were sentenced to death. That a priestess was no longer a virgin was believed to be indicated by the extinction of the sacred flame. While still living, the convicted Vestal was carried on a bier with all the formality of a funeral. Her friends and relatives joined the procession, mourning her. Dressed for burial, she was taken as far as the Colline Gate, placed in an underground cell prepared within the walls, and left to die. She did not receive a monument, funeral rites, or any other customary solemnities (Dionysius of Halicarnassus, *Antiquities* 2.67).

There were four major colleges of male priests: pontiffs, augurs, quindecimvirs, and a board of three men in charge of feasts (*tresviri epulones*) that was later increased to seven, and ultimately ten, because of the addition of new religious festivals. The method of selection to these priesthoods changed from time to time, varying between cooptation (selection by the surviving members to fill a vacancy) and a form of popular election. Records indicate that, during the republic, pontiffs and augurs came from leading noble families, usually assuming a priesthood at the beginning of a political career. For example, Julius Caesar, who came from an old patrician family, became a pontiff in his early twenties and was elected *pontifex maximus* even before he had held a major civic magistracy. Cicero, on the other hand, came from a provincial family and so lacked the initial connections that would have helped him gain access to a priesthood. He achieved political success through his skill as an orator, becoming consul in 63 BCE, and ten years later was admitted to the college of augurs.

The augurs controlled the auspices (*auspicia*), whereas the pontiffs were in charge of the sacred rites (*sacra*) or rituals (Cicero, *On the Nature of the Gods* 1.122). The duties of the augurs were to predict the anger of the gods, to inform those who conducted war or civic matters about the auspices and see that the auspices were obeyed, to observe lightning, and to keep all places of augural observation free and demarcated. Whatever an augur should declare to be unjust or unlawful, pernicious

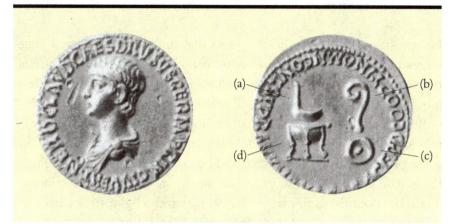

37. Gold coin issued by the emperor Claudius. On the reverse are depicted the sacral implements of the different priests: (a) an earthenware ladle, used for pouring liquids, the symbol of the pontiffs; (b) an augur's staff (*lituus*); (c) a libation bowl (*patera*), symbol of the priests in charge of feasts; (d) a tripod, symbol of the quindecimvirs. On the obverse, the young Nero is depicted, because Claudius had him made a supernumerary member of all four colleges, thus signaling the emperor's choice of successor.

or ill-omened, should be null and void (*On the Laws* 2.20–21). The importance attached to the taking of auspices is apparent in the story of Flaminius, the consul of 217 BCE, who, in his anxiety to assume his command as soon as possible, left Rome as a private citizen without taking the auspices or making the customary vows to Capitoline Jupiter (Livy 21.63). The senators questioned his action, saying that he did not hold proper authority or the right of auspices (Livy 22.1). Flaminius ignored this advice, and also some divine warnings; the results were the disaster at Lake Trasimene and his death. The dictator Fabius Maximus, himself an augur, convinced the Senate that Flaminius erred because of his neglect of the rituals and auspices rather than recklessness and ignorance (Livy 22.9).

The pontiffs' control of the rituals gave them general oversight of state religion, including religious festivals; maintenance of the calendar; and the publication of the *annales maximi,* a summary of the major events of each year that included wars, battles, grain shortages, famines, plagues, and prodigies. Writing in the late first century BCE, Dionysius of

Halicarnassus (*Antiquities* 2.73) reports that the pontiffs rendered judgments on all religious cases involving private citizens, magistrates, and religious officials. The pontiffs made laws for the observance of any religious rites that were not established either in writing or by custom. They scrutinized all magistrates who had responsibilities involving sacrifice or religious duty and all priests and their subordinates, to ensure there was no error in regard to the sacred law. The pontiffs' advice was sought by the Senate and put into effect by the magistrates or popular assemblies. Thus, the pontiffs' duties were both secular and religious; they became, as it were, a repository of both divine and human law.

The quindecimvirs supervised the performance of rituals (*quindecimviri sacris faciundis*). Originally the board consisted of two (*duoviri*), then ten (*decemviri*), fifteen (*quindecimviri*), and finally sixteen men, although

38. Augustan tripod base, with relief depicting a quindecimvir making a sacrifice on an altar, framed by two laurel trees.

the title *quindecimviri* was maintained. One of their duties was to guard the Sibylline Books, a collection of oracles and ritual texts written in Greek and kept in the temple of Jupiter on the Capitoline during the republic. They were also responsible for the admission of new oracles. Dionysius of Halicarnassus notes that the Senate ordered the quindecimvirs to consult the Sibylline Books and give advice "when political strife gripped the city, when a great calamity had happened in war, or when a portent or prodigy had appeared that was difficult to interpret" (*Antiquities* 4.62). In 399, because of plague, the Sibylline Books recommended a *lectisternium,* originally a Greek practice in which people entertained the gods at a banquet, placing their statues on couches in front of the temples. The board of two priests (*duoviri*) conducted the ritual in honor of Apollo, Diana, Latona (their mother), Hercules, Mercury, and Neptune (Livy 5.13).

The process of dealing with portents and prodigies illustrates the interaction of religion and politics. By strict definition, the term "prodigy" (*prodigium*) refers to a sign or portent that had been accepted by the state authorities as indicating that the favor of the gods (*pax deum*) had been broken or was about to be broken. When a particularly strange occurrence (for example, the birth of a two-headed calf or a hermaphrodite) was reported, the magistrate receiving the report would refer this event to the Senate, which would decide whether to acknowledge the phenomenon as a prodigy. This decision would be made in consultation with priests, many of whom also were senators by virtue of being ex-magistrates. The Senate would formally entrust the task of interpreting the prodigy to *haruspices* or, apparently in more serious cases, to the quindecimvirs, who would consult the Sibylline Books. The priests would present their findings to the Senate and propose remedial measures. The Senate would then instruct the magistrates or priests to carry out the prescribed expiation (Linderski 1995: 612–614). The Senate was thus able to control and even manipulate the report of a prodigy for political purposes, expediting or protracting the process as they saw fit. Writing in the mid-second century BCE, the Greek historian Polybius remarked on the utility of religion to the Roman state, concluding that it was *deisidaimonia* (fear, awe, or respect for the supernatural) which held the state together.

> In my opinion, the area in which the Roman constitution is most conspicuously superior is their concept of the gods. It seems to me that the very thing that is a matter of reproach among other peoples is what holds the Roman state together: I mean *deisidaimonia*. Religious matters are dramatized and introduced into their public and private life to such an extent that nothing could exceed them in importance. (Polybius 6.56)

Cicero regarded the prophetic warnings of the Sibylline Books and the advice of *haruspices* as a third category of Roman religious practice, the other two being ritual and the auspices (*On the Nature of the Gods* 3.5). *Haruspices* were diviners or seers who originally came from Etruria and were consulted by the Romans to deal not only with prodigies but more often with lightning and signs in the entrails of sacrificial animals. Loss of Livy's account of the early third century BCE prevents us from knowing precisely when it was that the Roman authorities began to consult these non-Roman seers, but the practice seems to have been established by the end of that century. A college of *haruspices* was only instituted in 47 CE by the emperor Claudius. Until then, *haruspices* apparently operated on a freelance basis, working for the state when requested, while generally offering their services to individuals.

In predicting from entrails the *haruspex* would stand with his right foot on the ground and his left on a stone (Figure 39) as he took the victim's liver in his left hand and "read" it. Any abnormality was thought to indicate disaster for the sacrificant or for the city as whole. In the case of lightning, the *haruspex* had to discern in which of the sixteen divisions of the sky the lightning had appeared and what it had struck. The lobes and other anatomical features of the liver were equated with regions of the sky, and certain areas were allocated to certain gods, who were thought to have influence over events that were discerned within their particular area.

39. The reverse side of a bronze mirror from Vulci depicts the mythical seer Calchas, dressed as a *haruspex,* examining a victim's liver. Etruscan, early fourth century BCE.

40. Model of an animal's liver from Piacenza in north Italy, used in divination by Etruscan seers. Divisions of the heavens are marked and identified on the model.

Not everyone, however, respected such predictions. Cato the Elder advised the bailiff of his farm not to consult a *haruspex,* augur, prophet, or astrologer (*On Agriculture* 5). Cicero recalled that Julius Caesar had disregarded the warning of a *haruspex* not to cross the sea to Africa before the winter solstice, noting that if he had not done so all his enemies would have gathered against him in one place. Cicero also noted that Cato expressed his amazement that one *haruspex* did not laugh when he saw another *haruspex,* recalling an anecdote about Hannibal who had advised a king to go war. When the king said that he did not dare to do so because the entrails forbade it, Hannibal asked, "Do you put more trust in pieces of ox meat than in a veteran commander?" (*On Divination* 2.51–53).

During the republic the interpretation of prodigies was a major factor in Roman politics; when the republican system of government collapsed, however, control of religion passed from the Senate to the emperor. Livy alludes to this change as he notes with apparent regret a disbelief in divine warnings, remarking that portents were no longer officially reported or recorded (43.13). Augustus, on becoming *pontifex maximus* in 12 BCE, burned more than two thousand prophetic writings and purged the Sibylline Books, transferring them to the temple of Apollo on the Palatine that he had built (Suetonius, *Augustus* 31). The following advice for Augustus, written by the Greek historian Dio from the vantage point of two centuries of hindsight, captures the essence of the religious policy of Augustus and his successors:

> Prophecy is essential, and so by all means appoint diviners and augurs to whom people who want advice on any matter will go. But it is appropriate that there should be no magic-workers (*mageutai*) whatsoever. For such men often incite many to revolution, either by telling the truth or, as more often, by telling lies. (Dio 52.36)

Although never officially accepted, astrology became increasingly popular, apparently supplanting other kinds of divination when control of religion shifted to the emperor (Barton 1994: 38). One of the earliest references to the presence of astrologers in Rome was made by Ennius who, in a list of religious hucksters, mentions "astrologers who hang around the circus" (Ennius, as quoted in Cicero, *On Divination* 1.132).

41. Mosaic from Bir-Chana, north Africa, third century CE, depicting astrological signs. At the center is a bearded bust of Saturn, surrounded by other planetary deities and the animals sacred to them. Around the edge are the signs of the zodiac. The intent of this mosaic was probably to ensure the lasting good fortune of the house in which it was situated (Dunbabin 1978: 161), thus reflecting a benign aspect of astrology.

And, as mentioned, Cato names the astrologer as one of the individuals that the bailiff of a farm must not consult (Cato, *On Agriculture* 5). In 139 BCE astrologers were expelled from Rome and Italy, "because they were profiteering by their lies and creating darkness in the minds of the fickle and stupid by their fallacious interpretation of the stars" (Valerius Maximus, *Memorable Deeds and Sayings* 1.3.3).

Tacitus reflected the state's ambivalence toward astrologers, as he deemed them "a breed of men untrustworthy for the powerful and deceitful for the ambitious, a breed that will always be both forbidden and retained in our state" (*Histories* 1.22). Although several emperors, including Augustus and Tiberius, used astrology for their own purposes, they were aware of the threat posed to their power when it was used by others. Suetonius reported that, after consulting an astrologer, Augustus had such faith in his own destiny that he published his own

42. Coin of Augustus with sign of Capricorn. (*Obv.*) Augustus as *divi f(ilius)*, son of a god; (*rev.*) Capricorn with globe between its feet and legend referring to Augustus being proclaimed as *imperator* (supreme commander) eleven times.

horoscope and issued silver coinage bearing the sign of the constellation Capricorn (Suetonius, *Augustus* 94). In noting the publication of this horoscope, Dio remarked that Augustus imposed restrictions on divination and forbade predictions to be given to anyone who was alone, especially prophecies concerning death (Dio 56.25).

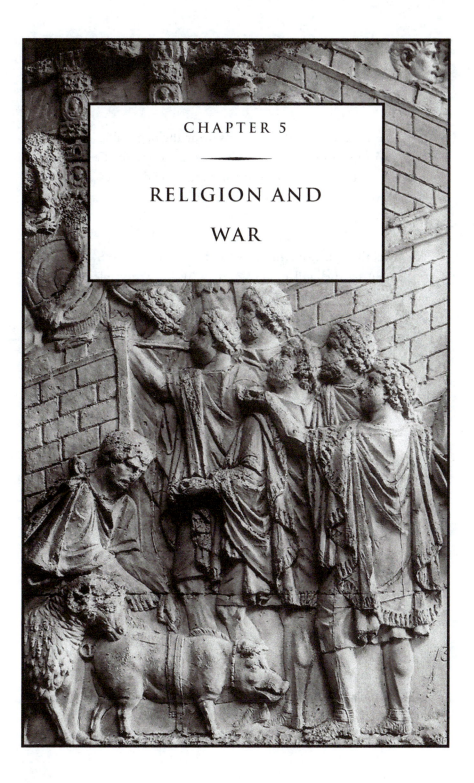

# CHAPTER 5

## RELIGION AND WAR

It will be apparent that the Romans made the beginnings of their wars and their motives for war in accordance with the utmost piety. And it was for this reason in particular that they had the gods on their side in times of danger. (Dionysius of Halicarnassus, *Antiquities* 2.72)

We owe the creation, increase, and retention of our empire (*imperium*) to the will of the gods....We have excelled every race and nation in piety (*pietas*), in respect for religious matters (*religio*), and in that singular wisdom which recognizes that everything is ruled and controlled by the will of the gods. (Cicero, *On the Reply of the Haruspices* 19)

As we saw in the previous chapter, the Greek historian Polybius (6.56) observed that the Romans' awe of the supernatural (*deisidaimonia*) held the state together. Dionysius of Halicarnassus, another Greek historian, remarks on the effectiveness of Roman piety in the initiation of wars. Cicero notes that the Romans owed their empire to their piety (*pietas*), a proper respect for religious matters (*religio*), and a recognition of the omnipotence of the gods' will. The basic concept of the Greek *eusebeia* and the Latin *pietas* is the dutiful and correct performance of the gods' worship. Nowhere in the surviving testimony is the Roman insistence on such piety better seen than in the conduct of their wars. At every stage of any military undertaking, from beginning to end, the gods' favor had to be maintained by the correct performance of various rituals, especially the taking of auspices. Success was attributed to the favor of the gods, whereas defeat was the result of a failure to gain that favor, as was apparent in the story of the death of Flaminius at Trasimene.

43. Trajan's Column in Rome. On this victory monument a spiraling frieze depicts the emperor Trajan's wars against the Dacians (101–106 BCE), including the rituals enacted at different stages of the campaign. The original statue of Trajan has been replaced by one of Saint Peter.

44. A scene from Trajan's Column showing the ritual purification of the army by means of a pig-sheep-bull sacrifice (*suovetaurilia*). The victims are being led by various attendants around the outside of the military camp and then through a gate (center). Inside the camp, Trajan is shown on the left, his head covered as he pours a libation. Facing him are a musician and soldiers carrying standards.

The Romans had special priests, fetials, whose duties included the declaration of war and the making of treaties. Dionysius of Halicarnassus thought it necessary to explain the extent and importance of the fetials' duties "so that those who are unaware of the piety (*eusebeia*) practiced by the Romans at that time may not be surprised that all their wars had a most glorious outcome" (*Antiquities* 2.72). In addition to discerning the need for the "utmost piety," he emphasizes the fetials' duty to ensure that Rome's wars were just:

> It is the fetials' duty to take care that the Romans do not under-take an unjust war against any city that is in alliance with them, and if others begin to break a treaty with them, to go as ambas-sadors and first make a verbal request for justice and then, if their demands are not obeyed, to sanction war. (Dionysius of Halicarnassus, *Antiquities* 2.72)

Originally, when Rome was warring against neighboring peoples, the fetial priests performed both ritual and diplomacy in the steps lead-ing up to the actual declaration of war, seeking reparation and calling upon the gods to witness that the Roman cause was just. But when wars were waged overseas against non-Italic peoples, these rituals were modified because of the distances involved in travel between Rome and the potential enemy. By the time of the mid-republic, the fetials were still consulted on ritual matters, but the practical details of diplo-macy were assigned to legates or ambassadors who were appointed by the Senate to conduct negotiations with foreign powers. In 200 BCE, before the motion to declare war on Philip of Macedon was put to the People's Assembly, sacrifice and prayers were offered by the con-suls. They reported that the gods had given their approval and that the victim's entrails portended an extension of territory, victory, and a tri-umph (Livy 31.5). After the People's Assembly had voted for war, the Senate consulted the fetials about the delivery of the actual declaration of war, asking whether it should be delivered to Philip in person or whether it was sufficient to announce it at the first fortified post in his territory. The fetials replied that whichever way it was done would be correct (Livy 31.8). Although we are not told which method was chosen, it later became the custom for a fetial to hurl a spear into an area near the temple of the war goddess Bellona that had been designated as enemy territory, a legalistic solution that avoided the fetials having to leave Rome.

Livy describes the spectacle of the consul's departure for war against Perseus of Macedon in 171 BCE:

> After making his vows on the Capitolium, the consul Publius Licinius set out from the city, wearing the general's cloak, the *paludamentum*. This event is always conducted with great dignity and solemnity; it especially attracts men's eyes and minds when they escort a consul who is going against an enemy that is great and renowned either for valor or good fortune.
>
> Not only concern for the man's office but also enthusiasm for the spectacle draw people together to see their leader to whose command and strategy they have entrusted the protection of all the state's interests. There come into their minds thoughts about the disasters of war, how uncertain is the outcome of fortune and how impartial is Mars, the god of war.... What mortal knows what is the mind-set or fortune of the consul that they are sending to war? Are they going to see him soon, as he climbs the Capitol with his victorious army into the presence of those gods from whom he departed? Or are they going to give joy to the enemy? (Livy 42.49)

Once war had started, morale had to be maintained both at home and in the field. Throughout his account of the long war with Hannibal (218–201 BCE), Livy's narrative of the crises and disasters is punctuated by reports of prodigies and their expiation. A long list of prodigies that occurred in the first year of the war concludes with the

45. Sacrifice on the departure from a port city, Trajan's Column. The emperor Trajan is pouring a libation, while opposite him a slave attendant leans forward over the victim at the edge of the wharf. Behind Trajan are two soldiers carrying standards. (Ryberg 1955:125–126)

authorial remark that the vows and expiations prescribed by the Sibylline Books went a long way toward freeing men's minds of their religious fears (Livy 21.62). Prior to the account of the Roman defeat at Lake Trasimene in 217 BCE, a list of portents includes javelins that burst into flames, shields sweating blood, soldiers struck by lightning, a rain of red-hot stones, waters flowing with blood, and several phenomena associated with the war god Mars (Livy 22.1). The Senate first decided that these were prodigies that must be expiated with sacrificial victims and a three-day *supplicatio*. Then, on the advice of the decemvirs who had consulted the Sibylline Books, it was also decreed that gifts be made to Jupiter, Juno, and Minerva, as well as offerings to Juno the Queen on the Aventine and Juno Sospita (the Protectress) at Lanuvium. The freedwomen were also to make a contribution to their patron goddess,

Feronia. The people of Rome had to do everything possible to expiate these prodigies and win back the gods' favor.

In the field, the consul Flaminius disregarded two omens just before battle. His horse stumbled and threw him, and a military standard could not be raised. Whereupon he cried, "Go, tell them to *dig* the standard out, if their hands are too numb with fear to pull it up!" (Livy 22.3). Flaminius was killed, the Romans were defeated, and a dictator was appointed to deal with the crisis. As we have seen, the disaster was attributed to Flaminius' neglect of the rituals and auspices. The Sibylline Books were consulted, a flaw was reported in the performance of a vow to Mars, and the ceremony had to be performed anew and on a larger scale. Other recommendations were a vow of games to Jupiter, temples to Venus Erycina and Mind, a period of public prayer (*supplicatio*), and a public banquet in honor of the gods (*lectisternium*). Finally, the Romans were to promise to sacrifice all the animals born in a certain spring, "if they should prove victorious and the state be in the same condition as it had been before the war" (Livy 22.9). The Romans were both pragmatic and legalistic in their dealings with the gods.

But these various expiations and vows apparently did not appease the gods. In the following year, Hannibal inflicted another defeat at the battle of Cannae. Livy reports that one consul, Lucius Aemilius Paullus, had wanted to delay the battle, but his colleague Varro gave the command to start; whereupon Paullus announced that the sacred chickens refused to eat. Varro recalled the recent disaster suffered by Flaminius and the defeat of Publius Claudius in the First Punic War. The latter had flung the chickens into the sea, declaring that if they would not eat, they would have to drink. And so Varro reluctantly ordered his soldiers back to camp for that day. But, as Livy remarks, "It was almost the very gods who postponed, rather than prevented, the destruction that threatened the Romans" (Livy 22.42). Reluctant or not, Varro obeyed the auspices – and survived. Paullus, however, did not. Cicero raises an awkward question when he remarks that Flaminius did not obey the auspices and consequently perished together with his army, whereas a year later Lucius Aemilius Paullus obeyed the auspices yet both he and his army died in battle (*On Divination* 2.71).

In the aftermath of the defeat at Cannae, Livy reports that the conviction of two Vestals for unchastity was regarded as a prodigy. To expiate this impiety and other prodigies, the Romans resorted to human sacrifice, an action Livy describes as un-Roman.

> In addition to these dreadful disasters, they were also terrified by a number of prodigies, especially because in that year two Vestals had been convicted of unchastity. Of these one had been buried alive, as the custom is, near the Colline Gate, and the other had committed suicide.... In the midst of so many misfortunes this act of impiety (*nefas*) was regarded as a prodigy, and so the decemvirs were ordered to consult the (Sibylline) books....
>
> In accordance with the books of fate, some unusual sacrifices were made: one of which consisted of the live burial in the Forum Boarium of a Gallic man and woman and a Greek man and woman, in a place walled in with stone which even before this time had been defiled with human victims – a most un-Roman practice. (Livy 22.57)

Victory, however, presented a very different scenario. The successful general would apply to the Senate for permission to celebrate a triumph, a spectacular victory parade. If permission was granted, the triumphal procession would begin outside the sacred boundary of the city (*pomerium*) near the temple of the war goddess Bellona, pass through the Circus Flaminius and Circus Maximus, then go round the Palatine Hill and through the Forum along the Sacred Way to the Capitoline, where it terminated with a sacrifice to Jupiter Best and Greatest. Displayed in the procession were the spoils of war, the captives, the victorious army, and the general himself, who rode in a special chariot that resembled a round tower.

46. Silver cup from Boscoreale depicting the future emperor Tiberius riding in the triumphal chariot.

A triumph was a spectacle for the whole city to enjoy, but it also had the effect of enhancing the political reputation of the general whose victory was being celebrated. As Rome conquered more and more territory, triumphs became more ostentatious, focusing on the triumphant general rather than on gratitude to the gods. Permanent victory monuments were erected, not only temples that had been vowed during the war but also, by the late first century BCE, triumphal arches that depicted the triumph itself and, later, victory columns of the emperors Trajan and Marcus Aurelius decorated with scenes from the wars they had fought.

The biographer Plutarch (c. 46–120s CE) describes the triumph of Lucius Aemilius Paullus after his victory in Macedonia in 168 BCE. The deposed Macedonian king Perseus and his family were obliged to march in the victory parade. Platforms were set up for people to view the

47. The triumphal arch of Trajan at Benevento, in south central Italy.

spectacle, which lasted three days. Two days were devoted to processions displaying the booty. Two hundred and fifty chariots transported statues, paintings, and colossal figures. Numerous carts carried the finest and richest of the Macedonian weaponry. Three thousand men carried silver coins in seven hundred and fifty vessels. Others carried engraved silver bowls, drinking horns, dishes, and cups.

On the third day, immediately at dawn, trumpeters marched out, playing not a march or processional tune, but the kind of sound that the Romans use to rouse themselves for battle. Following these came one hundred and ten stall-fed oxen with gilded horns, adorned with ribbons and wreaths. Leading the animals to sacrifice were young men wearing aprons with fine purple borders, and boys bearing silver and gold libation cups. . . .

Then came Aemilius himself, mounted on a magnificently

48. Three scenes from the triumphal procession depicted on the arch of Trajan at Benevento. *Above, top:* At the far right is a temple. From the right, two tunic-clad figures lead the procession, followed by a second pair carrying a large vessel of water or wine for the sacrifice. Next come two trumpeters, a horn blower, two *camilli* with shields, and then the sacrificial victims accompanied by attendants, one of whom has a pail for entrails balanced on his left shoulder. *Center:* From the left, two groups of victims with attendants, one with an ax and two carrying a pail. In front of them is a group of captives, led by soldiers and a *camillus* carrying a tablet probably giving the names and origins of the captives. *Bottom:* Amid the line of captives is another victim with attendants. At the center is a *ferculum,* a rectangular platform bearing a crown, carried by four tunic-clad attendants. Two more victims are at the far right. (Ryberg 1955:150–152)

adorned chariot, a man worthy to be beheld even without the trappings of power. He was dressed in a purple robe interwoven with gold, holding in his right hand a branch of laurel. The entire army also carried laurel, following the general's chariot in their companies and divisions. Some sang the traditional songs interspersed with ribaldry, others victory hymns and the praises of Aemilius, who was the object of everyone's gaze and admiration. (Plutarch, *Aemilius Paullus* 33–34)

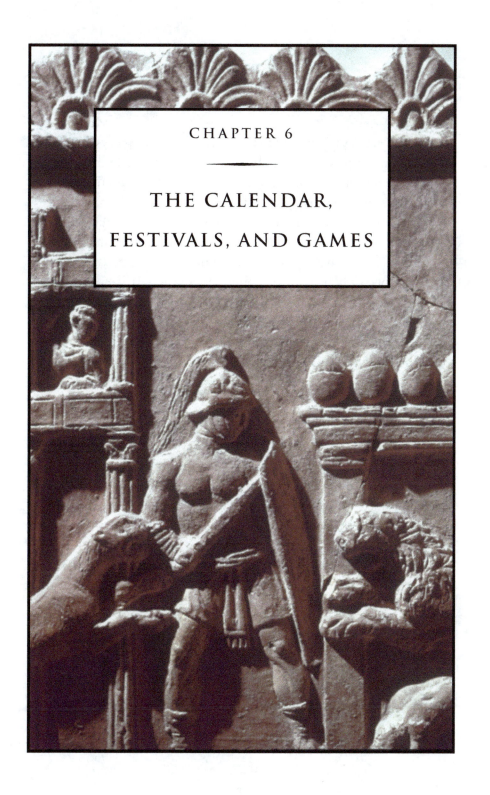

Festivals are days dedicated to the gods. On working days people may transact private and public business, and half-festivals are shared between gods and humans. But on festival days there are sacrifices, religious banquets, games, and holidays. . . .

The celebration of a religious festival consists of the offering of sacrifices to the gods, or the marking of a day by a ritual feast, or the holding of games in honor of the gods, or the observance of holidays. (Macrobius, *Saturnalia* 1.16.2–5)

There are as many days fixed for annual sacrifices as there are places in which they can be performed. (Livy 5.52)

T he official calendar was a basic Roman institution, regulated by the pontiffs and governing the timing of all state business. Several calendars inscribed on stone or painted on walls have survived, recording month by month the dates of the major religious festivals and the days on which assemblies could meet and justice be administered (BNP 2.60–77). During the republic the official Roman year consisted of 354 or 355 days, necessitating intercalation (the periodic insertion of an additional month) to keep the calendar in synchronization with the seasonal calendar and the solar year. Intercalation was neglected during the political disturbances of the 50s BCE and the civil wars that followed. Julius Caesar, as *pontifex maximus,* introduced a solar calendar that is still in use today, known first as the Julian calendar and later, after slight modifications introduced in 1582 by Pope Gregory XIII, as the Gregorian calendar.

The diversity and complexity of Roman festivals, in both public and private spheres, is apparent in Ovid's poem *Fasti,* an incomplete work that describes day by day the festivals of the first six months of the year. Most festivals honored one or more of the gods, while also offering a sense of community, relaxation, feasting, merriment, and entertainment in a carnival-like atmosphere. Ovid captures the carefree spirit of a festal day as he describes the festival of Anna Perenna, an obscure minor deity.

> On 15 March the merry festival of Anna Perenna is held not far from your banks, O Tiber. The ordinary people come and drink, scattered here and there on the grass, each with his own companion. Some are in the open air; a few pitch tents; there are those who make a leafy hut from branches; others set up poles in place of rigid pillars on which they spread and place their togas.
>
> But as they become warm with sun and wine, they pray for as many years as the cups they drink, counting as they drink.... There they sing songs that they learned in the theater, accompanying their words with ready gestures. Setting the wine bowl down, they perform vigorous dances, and a chic girl with streaming hair leaps around. As they return, they stagger about, making a spectacle of themselves, and the crowd that encounters them calls them blessed. Recently I ran into this procession, and I thought it worth telling. An old woman was dragging a drunk old man home. (Ovid, *Fasti* 3.523–542)

On 21 April the Romans celebrated the Parilia, a festival in honor of Pales, god of flocks and herds, that also marked the birthday of Rome. Part of the ritual involved bringing from the temple of Vesta the blood of the sacrificed trace-horse of the winning chariot in a race held on 15 October and the ashes of a cow in calf that had been killed at the festival of the Fordicidia on 15 April. These practices were evidently of great antiquity and were probably aimed at promoting the fertility of the land and flocks.

> Go, people, and bring from the virgin's altar the material for purification. Vesta will give them, and by Vesta's gift you will be pure. The material will be the blood of a horse and the ashes of a calf; the third thing will be the empty stalk of a hard bean. Shepherd, purify your well-fed sheep as dusk first falls. First sprinkle the ground with water and sweep it with a broom. Decorate the sheepfold with leaves and branches fastened on it. Adorn the entrance and cover it with a long garland. Make blue smoke from pure sulfur, and let the sheep bleat when she is touched by the smoking sulfur. Burn rosemary, pine, and juniper; let the laurel crackle as it singes in the middle of the hearth. Put a basket of millet with the cakes of millet; the country goddess takes particular delight in this food. Add her favorite meat and a pail of milk, and when the meat is cut up, pray to wood-dwelling Pales with an offering of warm milk. (Ovid, *Fasti* 4.731–746)

A similar rusticity is apparent in the ritual of the Matralia, a festival associated with women and with the birth and care of children, when mothers offered toasted cakes that had been hastily prepared and baked on a hearth (Ovid, *Fasti* 6.531–533). Another women's festival, the Matronalia, was on 1 March, the date of the dedication of the temple of Juno Lucina, goddess of childbirth. The cult title "Lucina" was thought to derive from *lux* (light), as Ovid implies when he bids the worshiper say, "Lucina, you have given us light, be present in response to the prayers of women in labor." Matrons thronged the goddess's temple, bringing flowering plants and wreathing their heads with flowers. Pregnant women, however, were warned to unbind their hair before praying, to ensure an easy delivery (Ovid, *Fasti* 3.251–258). On this day it was the tradition for husbands to pray for the health of their wives and give them gifts. Wives entertained their slaves and served food to them (Tibullus 3.1.3–4; 4.2.1).

Like the Matronalia, the Saturnalia (17–23 December) also featured a reversal of social roles, as masters waited on their slaves (Macrobius, *Saturnalia* 1.22–23). This festival in honor of the Italic god Saturn was described by the poet Catullus (14.15) as the "best of days." Coming at the time of the winter solstice, it was an extended period of rest, relaxation, and merrymaking. Even the stern and parsimonious Cato relented at this festival time and was willing to give his slaves an additional ration of wine (*On Agriculture* 57). The younger Pliny (61/62–c. 112 CE) retired to his garden apartment when the rest of his household resounded with shouts of festivity because of the seasonal license. In this way he did not interrupt the festivities, nor did they interfere with his studies (*Letters* 2.17). The poet Statius, writing in the late first century CE, declared that the Saturnalia would be as long-lived as Rome: "Time shall not destroy that sacred day, so long as the hills of Latium endure and while your city, father Tiber, and the Capitol remain" (*Silvae* 1.6.98–102). The Christian writer Tertullian (c. 160–c. 240 CE) complained that Christians were still observing the Matronalia and Saturnalia, festivals that he characterized as being all about gift giving, gambling, feasting, and noise (*On Idolatry* 14).

The major public festivals were funded by the state and organized by public officials, first the aediles and later, during the empire, a praetor. A festival would generally start with a procession that culminated in a parade of the gods' statues and ended with a sacrifice. Dionysius of Halicarnassus describes such a procession. First came the city's youth, followed by the contestants in the games that were an integral part of many major festivals. Then followed groups of elaborately dressed dancers, accompanied by flute players.

> After these dancers, a crowd of lyre players and many flute players paraded. Then came the men who carried the censers in which incense and perfumes were burned along the whole

route. Next came the men bearing the gold and silver vessels on display, both those that were sacred to the gods and those that belonged to the state. Last of all in the procession came the statues of the gods, carried on men's shoulders.... After the procession was over, the consuls and priests whose function it was sacrificed oxen. (Dionysius of Halicarnassus, *Antiquities* 7.72.13–15)

The gods were also honored by regular annual games, and by votive games that were generally onetime events vowed by magistrates or generals. At the beginning of the war with Hannibal in 218 BCE, there were just two sets of annual games celebrated in honor of Jupiter, the Roman Games and the Plebeian Games, held in September and November. In 212 BCE, votive games were held in honor of Apollo and were made annual four years later. By the end of the war, games in honor of the Magna Mater (Great Mother) and Ceres had been added, the former being made annual in 194 BCE. In the late first century BCE, seventeen days of the month of April were devoted to festivals that included games: seven to the Megalesia in honor of the Magna Mater, eight to the Cerialia in honor of Ceres, and two to the Floralia in honor of Flora, goddess of flowers and blossoms. The proliferation of festivals necessitated the appointment of officials to supervise all these ceremonies. In 196 BCE a college of three priests was instituted to organize the banquets that were offered at public festivals (Livy 33.42), a number that had increased to seven by the time of Augustus.

The games themselves were of two kinds, dramatic performances or stage shows (*ludi scaenici*) and horse and chariot races (*ludi circenses*). Plays were performed at various festivals, such as Plautus' *Stichus* at the Plebeian Games of 200 BCE and his *Pseudolus* at the Megalesia in 191 BCE. Such dramatic performances, however, were not to everyone's taste. In the prologue to Terence's *Mother-in-Law,* the producer tells how rival attractions had broken up two previous performances.

49. A theatrical comedy scene depicting (on the right) a master who is about to beat his slave. The masks worn by slaves conventionally portrayed them as ugly and often deformed.

For my sake, give a fair hearing to my request. I'm again intro-ducing Terence's play *Mother-in-Law* for which I haven't been able to get a quiet audience. Disaster has over whelmed it. Your understanding, however, and your support of my efforts will put an end to disaster. The first time I started to present this play, some famous boxers and then a tightrope walker caused a prob-lem. People formed claques; the uproar and shrieking of women forced me off the stage prematurely. So, in order to give this new play another chance, I started to use an old trick: I staged it anew. And I held the audience for the first act. But then a rumor spread that some gladiators were going to perform. The people flocked in, pushing, shouting, fighting for a place. In the mean-time, I couldn't hold my own ground. (Terence, *Mother-in-Law* 28–42)

50. A second-century CE funeral stele from Daldis (Turkey) erected by Ammias in memory of her husband, the Thracian gladiator Antaios who had probably named himself after the mythological giant Antaios, a wrestler who defeated and killed all his foes.

Another increasingly popular feature was the display of animals. As a result of Rome's overseas conquests, various exotic creatures such as elephants were exhibited, as well as indigenous animals like bears, bulls, stags, and boars. At the votive games given by the general Marcus Fulvius Nobilior after a victory in Greece, a panther and lion hunt was staged, and for the first time a contest of athletes was presented "as a spectacle" (Livy 39.22). Rivalry soon developed between the sponsors of the different kinds of spectacle, on the principle that the more expensive and elaborate the gift, the more the gods would be pleased and bestow their favor accordingly. In the increasingly politicized atmosphere of the later republic, both the aediles who organized the annual games and the victorious generals who sponsored votive games escalated their bids for the people's favor by providing bigger and better spectacles. The gods were still represented, but the officials who organized or sponsored the festivals were claiming the gratitude of the people for themselves rather than honoring the gods.

Aediles, elected officials who were at the beginning of their political careers, seized the opportunity for self-advertisement in order to attract future votes. As aedile in 65 BCE, Julius Caesar adorned the Forum and the Capitolium with temporary colonnades to display a mass of material that he was going to use in his forthcoming games. He produced wild animal hunts and games (*ludi*), some in conjunction with his colleague but others on his own (Suetonius, *Julius Caesar* 10). These productions would have been part of the state-funded *ludi,* but a gladiatorial show also mentioned by Suetonius would have been funded by Caesar himself, evidently from money borrowed from Crassus, the richest man in Rome. The investment paid off in 59 BCE, when Caesar became consul and formed with Crassus and Pompey the informal political coalition known as the First Triumvirate.

51. Terracotta relief from Campania showing gladiators and wild beasts (lion and lioness) in the arena.

In 55 BCE, Pompey held votive games in honor of Venus Victrix (Venus of Victory) at which he celebrated the dedication of Rome's first permanent stone theater. A temple to the goddess was incorporated into the seating area of the theater, thus including the goddess among the spectators. Cicero describes Pompey's games as the most elaborate and magnificent in the history of man (*Against Piso* 65). Dio reports that there were music and gymnastic contests, a horse race in the Circus, and the slaughter of wild beasts of many kinds. In five days five hundred lions were destroyed, and eighteen elephants fought against men wearing heavy armor. Some of these beasts were killed at the time; others evoked the pity of the crowd, and so were killed a little later (Dio 39.38). After his triple triumph in 46 BCE, Julius Caesar held games to mark the dedication of a temple to Venus Genetrix (Venus the Mother), from whom the Julian family claimed to be descended. In this way Caesar emulated Pompey's temple to Venus Victrix while also promoting his family's divine ancestry. These votive gifts were overwhelming in their magnificence, but such spectacular entertainment increasingly marginalized the religious aspect of the event.

At the traditional *ludi,* the gods still retained their place in the opening procession. After confessing that he has gone to the Circus Maximus more to be with his girlfriend than actually to watch the

52. Relief with scene depicting chariot racing in the Circus Maximus.

chariot races, Ovid describes the procession of the gods' statues, making appropriate comments on the different benefits bestowed by the various deities. The gods to whom he chooses to address his prayers are Venus, goddess of love, and Victory, as he fondly imagines that Venus' statue has nodded her assent to his prayer.

> But look, the procession's coming. Quiet everyone! Pay attention! It's time for applause. The golden procession is coming. First in the parade is Victory, her wings outstretched. Be on my side, goddess, and make my love prove victorious. You people who trust too much in the waves can applaud Neptune. I have no interest in the sea. I'm a landlubber. Soldier, you can applaud your god Mars. I hate warfare. Peace is my delight, and the love that is found in the midst of peace. Let Phoebus [Apollo] help the augurs, and Phoebe [Diana] the hunters. Minerva, turn the hands of the craftsmen to applauding you. Country dwellers, arise in honor of Ceres and Bacchus. Let the boxer propitiate Pollux, the horseman Castor. It's you that we applaud, sweet Venus, you and your Cupids with their bow. Nod in support of my undertaking, goddess, put the right idea into my girlfriend's mind. May she be enduring of my love. Look, she nodded and, by her movement, gave a favorable sign. I ask you to promise what the goddess has already promised. (Ovid, *Love Affairs* 3.2. 43–59)

During the empire, the games were monopolized by the emperors. Augustus states that he produced games twenty-four times in his own name, and twenty-three times in place of other magistrates; he also gave three sets of gladiatorial games (*munera*) in his own name and five in those of his sons or grandsons (Augustus, *Achievements* 22). Religious rituals continued, but increasingly the gods were overshadowed as emperors used such occasions for displays of their own munificence in order to maintain popular favor. The people's desire for entertainment and the emperors' exploitation of that desire became so excessive that in the early second century CE the satirist Juvenal could write with considerable truth that the people who had once voted for commanders, legions, and everything else now only desired two things: bread and circuses (*Satire* 10.78–81). In another satire (11.194–197) he wrote of the praetor who organized the Megalesian games: "There he sits, as if in a triumph, the prey of horseflesh. And if I may say so without offence to the huge and excessive mob, today the Circus holds all of Rome as its captive."

# CHAPTER 7

# OFFICIAL ATTITUDES

# TOWARD FOREIGN

# CULTS

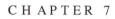

No individual shall take gods for himself, either new or alien ones, unless they have been recognized by the state. Privately they shall worship those gods whose worship they have duly received from their ancestors. (Cicero, *On the Laws* 2.19)

Notwithstanding the influx into Rome of innumerable foreigners who are under great obligation to worship their ancestral gods in accordance with the customs of their own countries, the city has never officially emulated any foreign practices. But, even though Rome has imported certain rites on the recommendation of oracles, she celebrates them in accordance with her own traditions, banishing all mythical mumbo-jumbo. (Dionysius of Halicarnassus, *Antiquities* 2.19)

In both republic and empire there are instances of the official adoption of new non-Roman gods, but often after initial resistance and unsuccessful attempts at suppression. The literary sources indicate that new cults were adopted by the state in times of crisis, especially plague or disaster in war. However, since the original infiltration of a new cult leaves little or no trace in the literary or archaeological record, it is quite possible that the literary record of the official adoption of a new cult merely indicates that the state authorities were sanctioning an already prevalent practice. Once a cult had taken hold of the populace, it generally would have been expedient to adapt it by eliminating unacceptable practices, rather than attempt to suppress it.

During a time of plague, the Romans vowed a temple to Apollo for the people's health in 433 BCE, and the temple was dedicated two years later (Livy 4.25 and 29). Apparently, however, Apollo was not a newcomer to Rome, since there was an earlier shrine to him in the area of a later temple (Livy 3.63) that was located outside the *pomerium,* the sacred boundary of the city, apparently because Apollo was a non-Roman god. There were prominent temples to Apollo both at Veii, an important Etruscan city to the north of Rome, and at Cumae in southern Italy. The cult adopted in Rome, however, was that of Apollo the Healer (Medicus), not the Greek god of prophecy worshiped at Cumae and also at Delphi.

During the siege of Veii in 396 BCE, the Romans performed the ritual of *evocatio,* the "calling forth" of an enemy's god to desert his or her homeland and come to a new abode in Rome. Through *evocatio* the Romans were depriving the enemy of divine protection while also admitting the enemy's god into their own pantheon. Livy describes the ceremony conducted by the general Camillus, who "evoked" Juno the Queen (Juno Regina).

> After taking the auspices, the dictator went out and ordered the soldiers to take up their arms. "It is under your leadership, Pythian Apollo, and inspired by your divine will," he said, "that I am advancing to destroy the city of Veii. To you I vow a tenth part of the spoils. To you, Queen Juno, who now dwell in Veii, I pray that you will accompany us in our victory to our city – soon to be your city – where a temple worthy of your greatness will receive you." After these prayers, he attacked the city from every side with vast numbers. (Livy 5.21)

After the fall of the city, the statue of Juno was ceremonially carried to Rome and housed on the Aventine Hill outside the *pomerium,* as was appropriate for a non-Roman deity.

The temple of Aesculapius, the Greek god of healing who was brought to Rome in 292 BCE, also was located outside the *pomerium.* This importation was enacted on the advice of the Sibylline Books during a time of plague. The god was brought from Epidaurus in Greece, allegedly in the form of a snake, which escaped from the ship and made its way to the Tiber island where a temple to the god soon was established (Livy 10.47.6–7; *Periocha* 11). That the Sibylline Books were the agent of change in the official adoption of a foreign god is an indication of the control exercised by the Senate and the religious authorities. Only the quindecimvirs had access to these books and, as noted earlier, consulted them on the orders of the Senate, a body that included a number of priests.

During the Second Punic War (218–201 BCE), when Hannibal invaded Italy, several religious innovations were made in response to prodigies that apparently coincided with military crises. The Sibylline Books recommended a number of expiations after the Roman defeat at Trasimene in 217 BCE, including the building of a shrine to Venus of Eryx, Eryx being a town in northwest Sicily whose principal deity, Astarte, was the Carthaginian equivalent of Venus. The importation of this foreign deity may be another instance of *evocatio,* though not explicitly mentioned as such by the sources (Livy 22.9; 23.30–31). The Romans probably feared the defection of this area of Sicily, which had been a stronghold of the Carthaginians during the First Punic War (264–241 BCE) (Orlin 1997: 108–109). Since her temple in Rome was located on the Capitoline Hill, Venus of Eryx is the first known example of a foreign deity to be brought inside the *pomerium.*

The Roman losses continued and the war dragged on, despite various appeals to the gods, including the institution of annual games to Apollo in 208 BCE during a time of plague (Livy 27.23). The Romans won a victory in 207 BCE, but Hannibal was still in Italy. In 205 BCE a prophecy in the Sibylline Books declared that, if ever a foreign enemy should invade Italy, he could be defeated if "the Idaean Mother of the Gods" were brought from Pessinus to Rome (Livy 29.10). This goddess, who was also known as the Mother, the Great Mother (Magna Mater), and Cybele or Cybebe, was worshiped extensively in Asia Minor (modern Turkey), in Sicily, and, indeed, throughout the Greek world. One of her most important sanctuaries was at Pessinus in Asia Minor, her priests were eunuchs known as Galli, and her cult was more exotic than was in accordance with traditional Roman religion.

53. A bronze Roman sculpture (c. second century CE) depicting Cybele enthroned on a cart drawn by two lions. The goddess wears a turreted crown, the symbol of her function as the protectress of cities. In her left hand she holds a tambourine or small drum (*tympanum*), and in her right a *patera,* a dish to hold offerings such as meal or wine.

In Livy's account of the goddess' arrival in Rome in 204 BCE, however, there is no sign of the exotic elements of her worship. On their way to collect the sacred stone that represented the goddess, the Roman envoys had stopped at Delphi in Greece, where the oracle declared that the goddess was to be welcomed in Rome by the best man in the city (Livy 29.11). A young noble, Publius Cornelius Scipio Nasica, received the goddess from the ship at Ostia, and gave her to the matrons to carry into Rome. Cybele was installed in the temple of Victory on the Palatine Hill (Livy 29.14), thus becoming the second known foreign deity to be brought within the *pomerium*. She was given a Romanized name, Magna Mater (Great Mother), and her reception was celebrated with a *lectisternium,* a ceremonial banquet for the gods, and new games that were given a Greek title, the Megalesia (Livy 29.14). Cicero notes that these games were "especially pure, sacred, and awesome (*religiosi*) both by custom and practice" (*On the Reply of*

54. Tomb portrait of a Gallus (second century CE). (a) Musical instruments characteristic of Cybele's cult: (on the left) a pair of cymbals, (on the right) a drum or tambourine (*tympanum*) and double Phrygian flute; (b) fillets or ribbons bound into the priest's curling braids; (c) a sprinkler for lustral water; (d) pectoral or breast plate, depicting Attis; (e) whip of knucklebones for self-flagellation; (f) box holding cult objects; (g) bowl of fruit with almonds (which are said to have sprung from Attis' blood when he castrated himself); (h) swathed dress, typical of female clothing. Ovid alluded to the Galli when he described a procession in honor of Cybele: "Her attendants howled, the frenzied flute blew, and unmanly hands beat the drums of bull's hide" (*Fasti* 4.341–342).

*the Haruspices* 24). Apparently the intention of the Roman authorities was to present the Magna Mater as Greek rather than Asiatic.

Dionysius of Halicarnassus notes that Rome "has never officially emulated" foreign practices but that such foreign rites as were introduced were celebrated "in accordance with her own traditions, banishing all mythical mumbo jumbo." The goddess' priest and priestess were

55. Terracotta statuette of Attis, Cybele's consort, seated on a rock and playing on a syrinx (shepherd's musical pipe). Hellenistic period from Macedonia.

Phrygian, and it was illegal for native-born Romans to celebrate her rites in the Phygian manner, "So careful is the state with regard to religious practices that are not indigenous" (*Antiquities* 2.19). However, the presence in the foundations of the original temple on the Palatine of some ninety figurines of Attis, the youthful castrated consort of Cybele, indicates that the Roman authorities failed to eliminate entirely the Asiatic elements of her cult (BNP 1.98). The inferior quality of these figurines suggests that they were private votive offerings from the poorer elements of Roman society. In the reign of Claudius (41–54 CE) restrictions on Roman participation in the rites of Cybele were relaxed, the quindecimvirs took part in her procession, and an additional festival, the Hilaria, was instituted in her honor.

Less than twenty years after the official reception of the Magna Mater, the Senate imposed severe restrictions on the worship of Bacchus, also known as Dionysus. Two major sources survive: a complex narrative by Livy, and a bronze tablet inscribed in archaic Latin that includes a letter addressed by the Roman consuls to Rome's Italian allies incorporating the senatorial decree. By the early fifth century BCE, the cult of Bacchus had been merged with that of Liber, an Italic deity. In the late third century BCE, references to Bacchus in the plays of Plautus indicate the Roman audience's familiarity with the god. By 186 BCE, as Livy notes, new manifestations of Bacchic worship had entered

56. Fresco from a *lararium* in the House of the Centenary in Pompeii depicting the god Bacchus, dressed in grapes, and holding a *thyrsus,* a long staff tipped with a pinecone, as he stands at the foot of Mount Vesuvius near Naples in Campania. This area is still noted for its wine.

Rome from Etruria and Campania. Originally, Bacchic rites had been restricted to women and initiations held only by day. A priestess from Campania, however, had started to initiate men, the rites were being held by night, and the number of initiation days had increased. Among the cultic excesses listed by Livy are the pleasures of wine, feasts, drunkenness, and promiscuity (Livy 39.8 and 13). Bacchic worship, as is apparent in Euripides' *Bacchae,* offered an intense and often ecstatic communion with the deity, involving an initiation ceremony, a ritual that set the initiate apart from the rest of society. Such practices, with their appeal to the individual as member of a group other than the civic community, were essentially un-Roman and, as such, inevitably aroused the suspicions of the state authorities.

The Senate treated the matter as a conspiracy (*coniuratio*), passing a decree that imposed strict controls on Bacchic worship both in Rome and peninsular Italy. No one was to conduct a Bacchic rite unless he had applied for permission to do so. Application had to be made to the city praetor, who would then refer the matter to the Senate, where there had to be a quorum of a hundred senators. The number of worshipers was restricted to five, thus undermining one of the basic appeals of Bacchic worship – mass participation by males and females in ceremonies that involved music, dancing, and the consumption of wine. There was to be no common fund, no official in charge of ritual, nor a priest. The authorities feared that organized meetings outside state control could prove politically subversive. Prescription of the death penalty indicates the gravity of the perceived threat.

The Senate ordered the destruction of Bacchic shrines in Rome and Italy, "except for any ancient altar or statue consecrated there" (Livy 39.18.7), thus sparing the shrines that had been established before the influx of the new forms of Bacchic worship. The intention was not to eliminate the cult completely but rather to impose stipulations that would curb the excesses that threatened traditional Roman religious practices. Moreover, complete suppression of the cult would have jeopardized the

57. Bronze inscription with the senatorial decree of 186 BCE suppressing Bacchic worship. This copy of the decree was set up in Bruttium in southwest Italy.

58. Fresco from the Villa of the Mysteries in Pompeii. From left to right: (a) a woman, a veil covering her head, observes the ensuing scenes; (b) a child reads from a papyrus, as a seated matron supervises the reading of what are probably ritual prescriptions; a young girl carries a dish of offerings to (c) a group of women making sacrificial preparations around a table; (d) Silenus, the traditional educator of Dionysus, playing a lyre, his gaze fixed on the scene of Dionysus opposite; (e) two women and sacrificial animals; a woman who appears terrified, perhaps at the sight on the opposite wall of the flagellation of a half-naked woman; (f) Silenus holding a bowl into which two satyrs gaze, one of whom brandishes a tragic mask; (g) Dionysus reclines in the lap of a woman, probably his bride, Ariadne; note the *thyrsus* (see Fig. 56), traditionally carried by Dionysus and his devotees. Some authorities interpret these scenes as representing the initiation into the cult of Bacchus/Dionysus; others suggest a marriage ceremony. On the difficulties of interpretation, see BNP 1.161–164.

*pax deorum.* As a result of the Senate's action, Bacchus' devotees were probably more discreet in their worship.

As the Roman Empire expanded throughout the Mediterranean world, the influx of foreign cults inevitably increased. The cult of the Egyptian goddess Isis was brought to Campania in the early first century BCE, probably by Italian merchants. This complex deity is invoked in Apuleius' novel *Metamorphoses* (also known as *The Golden Ass*) as "Holy and eternal protector of the human race, you who are ever beneficent in nourishing mortals, offering the sweet affection of a mother to the afflictions of the distressed . . ." (Apuleius, *Met.* 11.25).

59 (*left*). Polychrome statue of the goddess Isis, Roman, second century CE.

60 (*below*). Procession in honor of Isis, depicting cult officials carrying sacred objects. (a) A woman carries a rattle (*sistrum*) and a ladle for sacred water. (b) A senior official carries a sacred water vase in such a way that his hands do not touch the sacred object. (c) A sacred scribe with plumed headdress carries writing tablets. (d) A woman with a snake entwined around her arm carries a water bucket.

(a)      (b)      (c)      (d)

As with the worship of Bacchus, the cult of Isis involved initiation and offered a more personal appeal than traditional Roman religion, consequently encountering opposition from various authorities. During the politically turbulent years of the 50s BCE, orders were given to demolish shrines of Isis in Rome. In the late 40s BCE, however, the

61. Fresco from Herculaneum, near Naples, depicting Isis worship, perhaps at the spring festival of the Sailing of Isis. At the top of the steps, in front of a temple with a pair of sphinxes in front, stands a priest with a shaven head. He is carrying a golden vase, as described in Apuleius, *Met.* 11.11, which perhaps contained Nile water. He is flanked by a priest and priestess, each carrying a rattle (*sistrum*). On the other side of the sphinxes are palm trees and Egyptian ibises. At the foot of the steps a priest, also shaven, seems to be conducting a choir of both males and females. He, like the male figure at the top of the steps, is black, probably coming from southern Egypt. Another shaven priest is tending the flame on an altar. Mid-first century CE.

construction of a temple to Isis and Serapis, another Egyptian god, was authorized by Antony, Lepidus, and Octavian. But Antony's departure for Egypt, and his alliance with Cleopatra, put an end to this project. Private Isis worship evidently continued, for in 19 CE the emperor

Tiberius banned Egyptian cults in Rome. In 43 CE a temple of Isis and Serapis was officially established on the Campus Martius by the emperor Claudius, a grandson of Antony.

The cult of Mithras, who apparently derived from an Indo-Iranian deity, became popular throughout the Roman world from about 100 CE. He typically is depicted slaying a bull. Our main sources for the cult are archaeological, and the few literary references yield little information about its history. The cult was open only to men, was especially popular with the military, and had little appeal to the upper classes. The sanctuaries (Mithraea) were small, resembling caves that were decorated to represent the cosmos. Here initiates met in groups for a ritual meal.

62. Mithraic relief from Nersae in central Italy. Mithras, typically wearing a Phrygian cap, kills a bull. To the left of the raven perched on Mithras' cloak is the figure of the sun with a charioteer's whip. To the right of Mithras' head is the figure of the moon with a crescent moon and quiver. The two side panels apparently depict mythological scenes (see BNP 2.307–308).

63. Sanctuary of Mithras in the lower church of S. Clemente, Rome.

When the group expanded beyond a certain size, a new group would be organized to preserve the intimacy of the community. In this way the devotees probably avoided the problems encountered by the worshipers of Bacchus and Isis.

The influx of foreign cults into Rome ultimately proved uncontrollable. Writing in the early second century CE, the satirist Juvenal professes his xenophobia: "I cannot bear a Greekized Rome. And yet what proportion of our dregs comes from Greece? The Syrian Orontes has long since flowed into the Tiber, bringing its language and customs" (*Satires* 3.60–63).

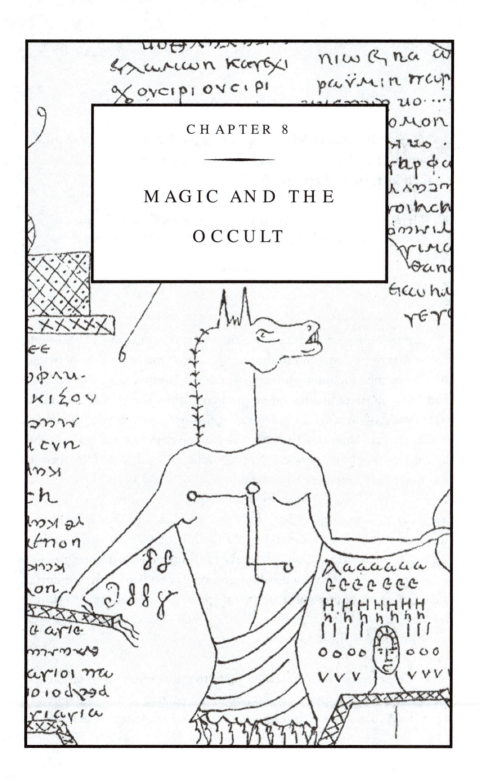

CHAPTER 8

MAGIC AND THE

OCCULT

Magic has certainly left traces among the Italic peoples too, in our Twelve Tables, for example, and in other sources. . . . (Pliny the Elder, *Natural History* 30.12)

There is no one who does not fear being spellbound by malevolent prayers. (Pliny the Elder, *Natural History* 28.19)

---

Examination of the ancient testimony from the mid-republic through the first three centuries of the empire reveals many variants of magic and the occult, including sorcery, witchcraft, incantations for healing, binding spells, necromancy (attempted communication with the dead), the wearing of amulets as protection against evil and disease, the interpretation of dreams, and astrology. These practices were at and beyond the fringe of traditional state and family religion, and so were perceived as a threat to the established order.

Our word "magic" derives from *magus,* a loanword from Persian originally meaning a fire priest, that came into Latin via the Greek *magos.* Apuleius, the late-second-century CE author of *Metamorphoses* or *The Golden Ass,* who himself was accused of magic (*mageia*), defines a *magus* as "someone who, through the community of speech with the immortal gods, possesses an incredible power of spells (*cantamina*) for everything that he wishes to do" (Apuleius, *Apology* 26.6). Cato the Elder records an incantation for healing a dislocation:

A dislocation can be healed with the following incantation (*cantio*): Take a green reed, about four or five feet long, split it down the middle, and let two men hold it against your hips.

Begin to chant: *motas vaeta daries dardares astataries dissunapiter.* Continue until the two halves of the reed come together. Wave a piece of iron over the reed. When the halves have come together and are touching one another, take the reed in your hand and cut it on the right and on the left. Bind it over the dislocation or fracture, which will then heal. Nevertheless, perform the following incantation for the dislocation every day: *huat haut huat ista pista sista dannabo dannaustra.* Or use this incantation for the dislocation: *huat haut haut istasis tarsis ardannabou dannaustra.* (Cato, *On Agriculture* 160)

But incantations were not always palliative. In addition to his remark that there is no one who does not fear being spellbound by malevolent prayers, Pliny the Elder cites two clauses from the laws of the Twelve Tables: "whoever shall have bewitched (*excantassit*)" and "whoever shall have cast an evil spell (*malum carmen incantassit*)" (*Natural History* 28.18–19). Such was the perception of the power of incantation that the death penalty was prescribed for anyone who cast spells upon another human being: "If any person has sung or composed against another person a song (*carmen*) such as was causing slander or insult to another, he shall be clubbed to death." Also in the Twelve Tables was a stipulation that no one should "take away the harvest of a neighbor by reciting spells."

Pliny tells of a freedman who was prosecuted for sorcery because he was more successful in farming than his neighbors. The charge was *veneficium* – literally, the making (*fic*) of *venenum* – the primary meaning of which is defined by the *Oxford Latin Dictionary* as "a potent herb or other substance used for medical, magical, etc., purposes," and is probably best translated as "potion" or "spell," though it can also mean poison or the use of poison as a criminal offense. Another meaning is "supernatural influence" since the root derives from *venus,* the original meaning of which was "propitiatory magic." Thus *veneficium* is often best translated as "sorcery" or "witchcraft."

Gaius Furius Cresimus, a freedman, reaped from a small field a harvest much more abundant than his neighbors did from their vast properties. He was much envied and suspected of having attracted the harvests of others by spells. So the curule aedile, Spurius Albinus, appointed a day for his trial. Fearing that he would be convicted when it came to a vote, Furius transported all his farming equipment to the Forum and brought in his entire household..., together with well-made tools, heavy pickaxes, weighty plowshares and well-fed oxen. Then he said, "Citizens, these are my evil spells. But I cannot show or bring to the Forum my late hours, my sleeplessness, and my sweat." He was unanimously acquitted. (Pliny the Elder, *Natural History* 18.41–43)

The connection between envy and bewitching with a malevolent glance or utterance is apparent in a poem of Horace in which he writes of his farm as a place where there is no one to diminish his comforts by a sidelong glance (*obliquo oculo*), or to poison or spellbind him with a bite of concealed hatred (*Epistles* 1.14.37–38). In two poems to his mistress, Catullus (5.12–13 and 7.12) expresses his fear that knowledge of the exact number of their kisses will enable someone to cast the evil eye (*malus invidere*) on them or bewitch them with an evil tongue (*mala fascinare lingua*). In a poem of Virgil, a shepherd says that love is not to blame for the emaciation of his sheep, but rather that "some eye (*oculus*) or other is bewitching (*fascinat*) my tender lambs" (*Eclogue* 3.103). Pliny the Elder writes of Fascinus (the phallus deity), who gives divine protection to children, a reference to the custom of hanging phallus effigies around the necks of babies to avert the evil eye. He also notes that the evil eye can be averted by spitting three times if a stranger arrives or a sleeping baby is looked upon (*Natural History* 28.39). The antiquarian Varro mentions a reference to amulets that were hung on boys' necks as prophylactics (*remedia*) to keep them safe (*On the Latin Language* 7.107). These several references by authors of the late republic and early empire attest to what probably were long-standing practices.

64. Roman mosaic, second–third century BCE from Antioch (Turkey), depicting the evil eye surrounded by its enemies: a raven, a trident and sword, a scorpion, serpent, dog, centipede, leopard, and a phallic dwarf. On such designs, intended to avert the evil eye, see Dunbabin 1978: 161–163.

Livy reports an incident in 331 BCE concerning the deaths of a number of prominent Roman men during a plague. Twenty Roman matrons, subjected to what apparently was trial by ordeal, died after drinking the potions (*venena*) they themselves had brewed. The potions are described as *medicamenta* that were said to be salutary (*salubria*). More women were convicted of *veneficium,* and the matter was treated as a prodigy and expiated (Livy 8.18). That the penalty was death is indicated by Valerius Maximus (*Memorable Deeds and Words* 2.5.3). These matrons may well have been the wives and other women-folk of prominent citizens who died from a plague that the women were attempting to cure. The charge of *veneficium* noted by Livy was probably brought under a law of the Twelve Tables concerning the use of potions or spells thought to have magic and thus curative powers. In 81 BCE a law was passed that made a distinction between *venena* and *mala* (evil) *venena;* this law also covered the making, selling, and possession of *mala medicamenta* (evil medications) with intent to kill (*Digest* 48.8.1–2; Dickie 2002: 145–146).

A frequent term of abuse in Plautus' plays is *veneficus* (feminine *venefica*), a practitioner of *veneficium,* and thus a sorcerer. In addition to the more common *veneficae,* some women practitioners of magic were called *cantatrices* (prophetesses, singers of spells), and *sagae* (wise women, who are often elderly). Originally these terms would have denoted distinct specialties, but later they became interchangeable. Horace characterizes the witches who used to haunt a former burying ground on the Esquiline Hill as "twisting men's minds with spells (*carmina*) and potions (*venena*)." He describes two particular witches and some of their practices, including that of necromancy. They dug up the earth with their nails and tore a black lamb to pieces with their teeth, pouring the blood into a trench to summon the ghosts of those they wanted to question (*Satire* 1.8).

Apuleius gives a particularly gruesome description of a witch's workshop:

> First she arranged her deadly laboratory with its customary equipment, setting out spices of all sorts, unintelligibly lettered metal tablets, the surviving remains of ill-omened birds, and numerous pieces of mourned and even buried corpses; here there were noses and fingers, there spikes covered with flesh from crucified bodies, elsewhere the preserved gore of murder victims and mutilated skulls torn from the teeth of wild beasts. Then, after reciting an incantation over pulsating entrails, she made offerings of various liquids. . . . Next she bound and knotted together hairs [stolen from a young man whom she desired] into interlocking braids and put them to burn on live coals along with several kinds of incense. (Apuleius, *Metamorphoses* 3.17–18)

The "unintelligibly lettered metal tablets" were probably *defixiones,* written spells intended to bind or tie and thus immobilize an individual, and *devotiones,* spells that vowed or consigned the victim to the powers of the underworld. These curse tablets, as they are generally known, were most commonly inscribed on lead, a dark-colored metal appropriate to the underworld powers, pierced with one or more nails, and placed in wells, fountains, or graves. Spells intended to sabotage horses and their charioteers at the circus games have been found deposited at turning points of the race track, where the danger was greatest. In the first of the following inscriptions, two racing teams are identified by the color under which they raced, and the driver's names are specified in order to ensure the spell's success.

> I call on you, demon, whoever you are, and ask that from this hour, from this day, from this moment, you torture and kill the horses of the Green and White teams, and that you kill and crush the drivers Clarus, Felix, Primulus, and Romanus, and that you leave not a breath in their bodies. (*ILS* 8753)

> I call on you, demon, who lie here [in the grave from which the text comes]: I deliver these horses to you so that you hold them back and they get tangled up [in their harness] and are unable to move. (Graf 1997: 155)

The power of spells is exemplified in Tacitus' report of the death of Germanicus, the emperor Tiberius' designated heir, who believed that he had been put under a spell by the governor of Syria, Gnaeus Calpurnius Piso.

> The cruel force of his disease was intensified by Germanicus' belief that Piso had put him under a spell (*venenum*). Examination of the floor and walls of his room revealed the remains of human bodies, spells (*carmina*), curses (*devotiones*), the name

of Germanicus inscribed on lead tablets, partially burnt ashes smeared with blood, and other devices of evil that are believed to consecrate souls to the powers of the underworld. (Tacitus, *Annals* 2.69)

The political repercussions of Germanicus' death were even more disturbing. Martina, a woman who "was infamous for her poisonings and

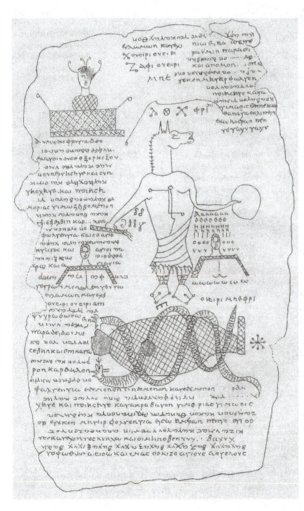

65. Drawing of the first side of a lead curse tablet from a tomb beside Appian Way, c. 400 CE. The horse-headed figure probably represents a horse-spirit connected with the circus. The mummified figure entwined by two fanged snakes represents the target of the spell, probably a rival charioteer, duly killed and buried. At the top left, the Egyptian god Osiris is shown emerging from his tomb. (Gager 1992: 67–72)

was dear to Plancina" (Piso's wife), was sent to Rome by the new governor of Syria, but died suddenly at Brundisium. Poisoning was suspected and foul play implied (Tacitus, *Annals* 2.74; 3.7). On his return to Rome, Piso was put on trial, committed suicide, and a senatorial decree concerning his trial and disgrace was distributed throughout the empire.

Curse tablets have been found throughout the Roman Empire but no remains from the republic or early empire have yet been found in Rome itself. Recently, however, a cache of "voodoo dolls" and lead curse tablets dating to the fourth century CE was discovered in the Piazza Euclid among the ruins of a fountain dedicated to the minor deity, Anna Perenna. A witch or sorceress was evidently manufacturing her magic wares, much in the manner described above by Apuleius. Many of the dolls were in lead canisters, on one of which the thumbprint of a woman has been detected. A high proportion of the erotic curses are aimed at women, but further cleaning and conservation could reveal curses against athletes or politicians (Faraone 2003: 48–53).

In the following binding spell from the Roman province of Egypt, one Theon attempts to make Euphemia fall in love with him:

> Seize Euphemia and lead her to me, Theon, loving me with mad desire, and bind her with shackles that cannot be loosed, strong ones of adamantine, for the love of me, Theon. Do not allow her to eat, drink, obtain sleep, jest or laugh but make her leap up out of every place and house, abandoning her father, mother, brothers, and sisters until she comes to me. . . . Burn her limbs, liver, female body, until she comes to me, Theon, loving me. . . . If she holds another man in her embrace, let her cast him off, forget him, and hate him; but let her feel affection for me, giving me her property, and doing nothing against my wishes. Holy names, here, and powers, here, enforce this spell and bring it to fruition, now, now, quickly, quickly. (Ogden 2002: no. 207)

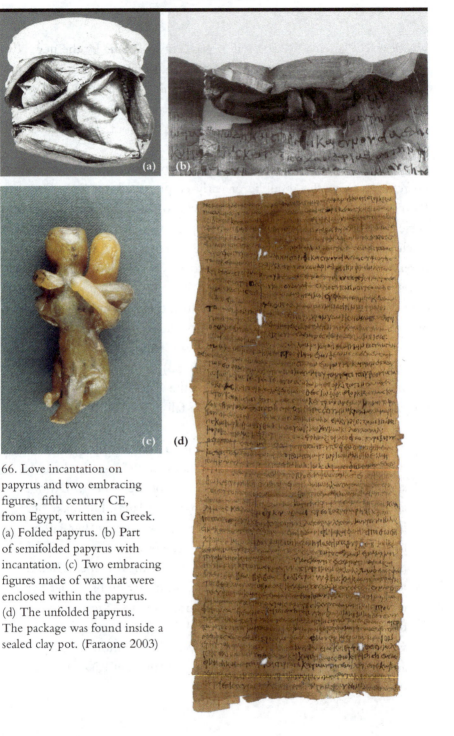

66. Love incantation on papyrus and two embracing figures, fifth century CE, from Egypt, written in Greek. (a) Folded papyrus. (b) Part of semifolded papyrus with incantation. (c) Two embracing figures made of wax that were enclosed within the papyrus. (d) The unfolded papyrus. The package was found inside a sealed clay pot. (Faraone 2003)

An unnamed individual dedicates Ticene, a woman who has probably rejected him, to the powers of the underworld, invoking them to immobilize specific parts of her body:

> Spirits of the underworld, if you have any power, I consecrate and hand over to you Ticene, the daughter of Carisius. Whatever she does, may it all turn out badly. Spirits of the underworld, I consecrate to you her limbs, her complexion, her figure, her head, her hair, her shadow, her brain, her forehead, her eyebrows, her mouth, her nose, her chin, her cheeks, her lips, her breath, her neck, her liver, her shoulders, her heart, her lungs, her intestines, her stomach, her arms, her fingers, her hands, her navel, her bladder, her entrails, her thighs, her knees, her calves, her heels, her soles, her toes. Spirits of the underworld, if I see her wasting away, I swear that I will be delighted to offer a sacrifice to you every year. (*CIL* 10.8249)

Fragments of otherwise lost works of poets indicate that love philters, or potions, were known and used in Rome in the late second

67. Terracotta figurine of a woman bound and pierced with needles, the intended victim of a spell. Egyptian, Roman period.

century BCE. Horace describes witches burying a young boy with his head protruding from the ground in order to use his liver as a love philter once he has starved to death (*Epode* 5). A passage from Virgil is the earliest extant allusion to misgivings about the use of such magic, as the lovesick Dido calls the gods to witness that she has reluctantly resorted to the magic arts (*magicae artes*) in the hope that they will return Aeneas to her or release her from loving him (*Aeneid* 4.478–493). But in his *Art of Love,* a treatise on how young men can secure and retain the affections of girls, Ovid categorically rules out the use of herbs, incantations, and love philters, because the first two do not work and love philters damage the mind and cause madness. His final advice is to avoid all actions that are unlawful (*Art of Love* 2.99–107).

CHAPTER 9

BECOMING A

GOD

He seems to me to be the equal of a god, he seems to surpass the gods, if it is right (*fas*) to say such a thing. (Catullus 51.1–2)

I always thought of you as a god whenever you speak. (Cicero, *On the Orator* 1.106)

O Meliboeus, it is a god who has fashioned this peace (*otium*) for us. For me he will always be a god (*deus*), and a tender lamb from my folds will often stain his altar. For he has allowed my cattle to wander, and me to play what I want on my rustic pipe. (Virgil, *Eclogue* 1.6–10)

---

The poet Catullus speaks of a man seeming to surpass the gods. The more prosaic Cicero has the famous orator Mucius Scaevola say that he has always thought of another orator, Licinius Crassus, as a god whenever Crassus speaks. Virgil goes further. Without naming Octavian, he calls the man who has brought peace (*otium*) a god – and then declares that Octavian will always be a god to whom he, Virgil, will pay cult with tender lambs from his folds, because he can compose verses now that his cattle are allowed to wander – a probable allusion to the restoration of Virgil's property that had been confiscated by the triumvirs (*Eclogue* 1.6–10). Poetic hyperbole this may be, but Virgil, unlike Catullus, did not feel it necessary to add any caveat such as "if it is right to say such a thing."

It was not unprecedented to hail men of power in terms of the divine, and even to pay them cult during their lifetimes. Shortly before Virgil's extolling of Octavian, the assassinated Julius Caesar had been declared a god, *divus Julius*. The epithet *divus* denoted a mortal who had become a god, like the Greek hero Hercules, in contrast to a *deus* like Jupiter or Mars (Price 1984: 220).

In the first two centuries CE most emperors were officially declared gods after their deaths. The origins of this practice lie both in Roman tradition and in Rome's contacts with the eastern Mediterranean world during the late third and early second centuries BCE. As we saw in Chapter 3, cult was paid at ancestors' tombs at the festivals of Parentalia and the Feralia. Ancestors were memorialized in the family home, their masks (*imagines*) kept in the *atria* and worn at funerals by relatives who impersonated the illustrious dead. In the Roman triumph, the victorious general impersonated the god Jupiter – albeit for only one day. From these traditionally Roman practices, it was but a short step to pay cult to a human being, even during his lifetime.

Many peoples of the Near East were accustomed to regard their rulers as gods, a well-known example being the Egyptian pharaohs. When Alexander the Great (356–323 BCE) overthrew the Persian Empire, the conquered peoples expected him to accept the same divine honors they traditionally accorded their rulers. Two stories circulated in the Mediterranean world: one that Zeus had entered the bed of Alexander's mother, Olympias, in the form of a snake; the other that the oracle of Zeus Ammon in Egypt had greeted Alexander as the son of Zeus (Plutarch, *Alexander* 2, 3, 27, 28). Two legends about Scipio Africanus, the Roman general who defeated Hannibal in 202 BCE, were apparently influenced by the Alexander tradition. Like Olympias, Scipio's mother was reputed to have had been impregnated by a snake, and Scipio himself was said to have cultivated a special relationship with Jupiter Capitolinus by spending part of the night in the shrine on the Capitol, "as if consulting with Jupiter on matters of state" (Gellius, *Attic Nights* 6.1.1–6). Also, in the early second century BCE, the city of Chalcis in Greece granted cultic honors to Titus Flamininus, the Roman victor over Philip V of Macedon. These honors were still being celebrated some three hundred years later, invoking Flamininus as Soter, protector or savior of the city and its people (Plutarch, *Flamininus* 16.3–4).

The story that Rome's founder became a god dates at least to the late third century BCE, the earliest extant reference occurring in Ennius' *Annales*. Livy gives a graphic though somewhat skeptical account of Romulus' death, his assumption into heaven, and his deification:

> Romulus was holding an assembly of the people on the Campus Martius to review the army when suddenly a storm arose with loud claps of thunder, enveloping him in a cloud so dense that it hid him from the view of the people. Thereafter Romulus was no longer on earth. The Roman people finally recovered from their panic when a bright and sunny day returned after the storm.
>
> When they saw that the king's seat was empty, although they readily believed the assertion of the senators who had been standing nearby that he had been snatched up on high by the storm, they nevertheless remained sorrowful and silent for some time, stricken with fear as if they had been orphaned. Then, on the initiative of a few men, they all decided that Romulus should be hailed as a god, son of a god, king and father of the city of Rome. With prayers they begged his favor (*pax*), beseeching him to be willing and propitious toward the Roman people and to protect their descendants forever. There were some even then, I believe, who privately claimed that the king had been torn into pieces by the hands of the senators.... (Livy 1.16)

This account has parallels with the assassination of Julius Caesar by his fellow nobles and his subsequent deification. At the time of his death in 44 BCE, Caesar was *pontifex maximus*, augur, consul for the fifth time, and dictator for life. By building a temple to Venus Genetrix (Venus the Mother), he had conspicuously asserted the claim that the Julian family was descended from Venus, the mother of Aeneas who fled from Troy to Italy. He also had the goddess' image displayed on coins – a medium that would reach a larger number of people than

68. (a) Denarius of Julius Caesar, 47/46 BCE: (*obv.*) Head of Venus; (*rev.*) Aeneas shown bearing his father, Anchises, on his shoulders and carrying the Palladium (the statue of Athena) in his right hand as he escapes from Troy. Note the legend CAESAR linking Julius Caesar with his legendary ancestors. (b) Denarius, 44 BCE: (*obv.*) Head of Caesar, wreathed, with the star symbolizing Caesar's deification and the legend CAESAR IMP[ERATOR] (commander-in-chief); (*rev.*) Venus holding the winged goddess Victory in her right hand, a scepter in her left. P. SEPULLIUS MACER is the issuer of the coin.

would ever see Caesar himself or his benefactions in Rome. He had celebrated four triumphs and been granted the privilege of wearing the garb of a triumphing general on all public occasions. This honor had earlier been granted to Lucius Aemilius Paullus, the victor over Perseus of Macedon in 167 BCE, and more recently to Pompey after his victories in the east, thus extending the association of the human and the divine beyond the day of the actual triumph.

Cicero, in a speech delivered in late 44 BCE, made a bitter reference to the deified Julius (*divus Julius*) being granted a special priest (*flamen*) and other honors pertaining to divine status (*Philippic* 2.110). After Caesar's assassination in March 44 BCE, his nineteen-year-old great-nephew Octavian had been declared Caesar's adopted son. His full title was now Gaius Julius Caesar Octavianus, and on his coins he styled himself as Caesar. The young man had not been slow to act on behalf of his dead father and, of course, himself. Pliny the Elder preserves a statement from Augustus' own memoirs, written some twenty years after the event, relating how a comet appeared at the games that Octavian was celebrating in honor of Venus Genetrix a few months after Caesar's death:

The common people believed that this star signified that the soul of Caesar had been received among the spirits (*numina*) of the immortal gods. And so the emblem of a star was added to the head of a statue of Caesar that I (Augustus) dedicated soon afterward in the Forum. (Pliny, *Natural History* 2.93–94)

After feuding with Antony, who had taken charge after Caesar's death, Octavian raised a private army, seized the consulship by threat of force, and joined with Antony and Lepidus, the new *pontifex maximus,* to form the Second Triumvirate. In January 42 BCE, Julius Caesar's divinity was acknowledged by the Senate and Roman people, and it was probably at this time that Octavian began to style himself as the son of a god (*divi filius*). Dio writes that the triumvirs laid the foundations of a shrine to the deified Julius Caesar in the Forum and had an image of him, together with one of Venus, carried in the procession at the circus games. They forced everyone to celebrate Caesar's birthday by wearing laurel and by merrymaking, forbidding any likeness of him to be carried at the funerals of his relatives, "just as if he truly were a god" (Dio 47.18.4–19.2).

Before the age of thirty, Octavian had acquired three major priest-hoods, becoming pontifex in 48, augur c. 41, and quindecimvir c. 37

69. Two silver denarii of Octavian styling himself as Caesar, son of a god (CAESAR DIVI FILIUS), minted for distribution to Octavian's troops sometime before 31 BCE. Octavian was continuing Julius Caesar's practice of asserting the Julian family's divine ancestry while also introducing new divine associations. (a) (*obv.*) Head of Octavian; (*rev.*) Venus holding the arms of Mars, father of Romulus. CAESAR DIVI F[ILIUS]. (b) (*obv.*) Head of Victoria (Victory); (*rev.*) Octavian posing as Neptune, with symbols of power and dominion in his hands and his foot on the globe, an allusion to his naval victory over Sextus Pompey, a son of Pompey the Great. Legend: CAESAR DIVI F[ILIUS].

BCE. On his return to Rome after his victory at Actium over Antony and Cleopatra, the Senate granted him a number of extraordinary honors. In addition to the usual prayers on behalf of the people and Senate, priests and priestesses were to offer prayers on Octavian's behalf, and everyone was to pour a libation to him at both public and private banquets, and pay cult to his Genius (Dio 51.19). In 27 BCE he assumed the title "Augustus," a name that derives from an adjective originally denoting a place that had been consecrated by augurs (literally "well-augured"), thus recalling the foundation of Rome by Romulus. Writing in the late second century CE, the historian Florus remarked that the very name and title raised him to the level of a god (Florus 2.34.66).

70. Statue of Augustus in a toga, his head covered as a sacrificant. Of Augustus' appearance, Suetonius remarked: "He had clear, bright eyes, in which he wanted people to think that there was a kind of divine power" (*Augustus* 79).

In an ode written in anticipation of Augustus' return from Gaul in 13 BCE, Horace pictures a farmer joyfully coming home from his vineyard to a feast and paying cult to Augustus as a god: "You with many a prayer, you with pure wine poured from the bowl, the farmer worships, mingling your godhead (*numen*) with that of the Lares" (*Odes* 4.5.31–35). Augustus was clearly treading a fine line in his acceptance of cultic honors. Though he himself was not a god, merely the son of a god, he was being worshiped via his numen and also his Genius.

On his return from Gaul, Augustus vowed to establish an altar to the Augustan Peace in the Campus Martius. A further step in his takeover of the state religion was marked by his assumption of the position of *pontifex maximus* on the death of Lepidus, who had continued to hold that office even though long exiled from Rome. Dio also notes that Augustus made part of his house on the Palatine public property (Dio 54.27). A new shrine to Vesta in his own house enabled him to

71. Altar of Augustan Peace (Ara Pacis Augustae), Rome. This monument was dedicated in 9 BCE. The actual altar is inside the marble enclosure. Depicted on the upper frieze of the sides of the enclosure are a procession of magistrates, priests, and the imperial family (see Figs. 21 and 33).

perform his duties as *pontifex maximus* and honor Vesta without having to go to the goddess' original temple in the Forum. Ovid honors the Palatine Vesta, referring to Augustus as one of three gods within his Palatine house:

> This is what the Senate has justly decreed. Phoebus [Apollo] holds a part, a second part has been given over to Vesta, what remains, he himself [Augustus] holds as the third party. . . . A single house holds three eternal gods. (Ovid, *Fasti* 4.950–954)

Among the temples that Augustus had constructed was the temple of the Lares on the Velian Hill (*Achievements* 19). Lares had long been worshiped in shrines at crossroads (*compitalia*), but most of these shrines had fallen into disuse during the late republic. Soon after becoming *pontifex maximus,* Augustus reorganized the city and integrated the worship of these Lares and his own Genius into the newly constituted two hundred and sixty-five wards (*vici*). In writing of 1 May, Ovid notes that this day "saw the foundation of an altar to the Guardian Lares and the gods' statuettes." At the conclusion of his notice of this festival, he remarks:

> In the city there are a thousand Lares and the Genius of the leader. He [Augustus] handed them over to the city, and the wards (*vici*) now worship three divinities (*numina*). (*Fasti* 5.129–130, 143–146)

Although his Genius was worshiped in Rome and he received cultic honors in many provinces, Augustus was not formally deified until after his death in 14 CE, when a temple and deification were decreed in his honor (Tacitus, *Annals* 1.10). Two centuries later Dio comments on the beginnings of imperial cult:

> Augustus meanwhile allowed precincts in Ephesos and Nicaea to be dedicated to Roma and to his father Caesar, naming him

72. Augustus as augur, holding a *lituus,* from an Altar of the Lares from the Vicus Sandalarius: (*left*) Gaius or Lucius Caesar (Augustus' grandsons); (*right*) a female member of the imperial family, probably Julia (Augustus' daughter) portrayed as Venus. Near Augustus' right foot is an augural bird. (Zanker 1988: 125)

73. Detail of a sacrificial procession, with attendants of a sanctuary of the Lares carrying statuettes of the Lares and the Genius of Augustus. (Zanker 1988: 129–134)

the hero Julius. . . . He ordered the Romans living there to honor
these divinities. But he permitted foreigners, whom he called
Greeks, to consecrate precincts to himself – the Asians in Perg-
amon and Bithynians at Nicomedia. That is where this practice
started and has been continued under other emperors, not only
among Greek nations, but among others subject to Roman rule.
(Cf. Figure 6, "Maison Carrée" at Nîmes)

74. Gemma Augustea, made for Augustus, c. 10 CE, showing him seated in the
guise of Jupiter with the goddess Roma beside him. In his left hand he holds the
*lituus,* the augural staff which symbolizes his high military command. Augustus'
gaze is directed toward Tiberius, who is descending from a chariot driven by
Victory. Between Tiberius and Roma is the young Germanicus, armed. To the
right of Augustus' head is a representation of Capricorn. Beneath his seat is an
eagle, the bird of Jupiter. Below, Roman soldiers and subjugated barbarians.
(Zanker 1988: 230–238)

In Rome itself and the rest of Italy, no emperor, no matter how worthy of renown, has so far dared to do this. However, when they die, those that ruled with integrity are also granted various divine honors in Rome and *heroa* (shrines to heroes) are built to them. (Dio 51.20.6–8)

The new emperor Tiberius, however, avoided the cultic honors that his predecessor had so assiduously fostered, forbidding temples or priest-hoods to be established in his name and statues or busts to be set up without his permission, only allowing such honors if they were not placed among the gods' images. He also vetoed a proposal that months be renamed after him and his mother, Livia, Augustus' widow (Sueto-nius, *Tiberius* 26), although that had been done for Julius Caesar and Augustus. Livia, however, was made a priestess of the deified Augustus, and she and Tiberius were responsible for the construction of a shrine

75. Cameo depicting Livia gazing at a statue of the deified Augustus. She holds wheat and poppies, symbols of Ceres, and wears the turreted crown of Cybele, with whom she was also identified. (Zanker 1988: 234–235)

76. Statue of the emperor Claudius in the guise of Jupiter, with eagle.

to her husband (Dio 56.46). On her death in 29 CE, Tiberius forbade her deification (Tacitus, *Annals* 5.2; Dio 58.2). Later, however, she was granted divine honors by her grandson the emperor Claudius (Suetonius, *Claudius* 11), the first time a woman had been so honored.

77. Apotheosis of the emperor Antoninus (138–161 CE) and his wife, Faustina. A nude winged figure transports the couple to the heavens. The emperor carries a scepter topped by an eagle. Two birds, restored as eagles, flank the emperor and his wife. Eagles were released from the top of the funeral pyres of emperors and were thought to carry the deceased's soul to heaven. The seated figure on the right wearing military dress is probably the goddess Roma.

After the deification of Augustus, all but the most egregiously bad emperors, like Caligula (37–41 CE), Nero (54–68 CE), and Commodus (180–192), were deified. When he realized he was dying, the emperor Vespasian, noted for his wit, is reported to have said, "O dear, I think I'm becoming a god" (Suetonius, *Vespasian* 23).

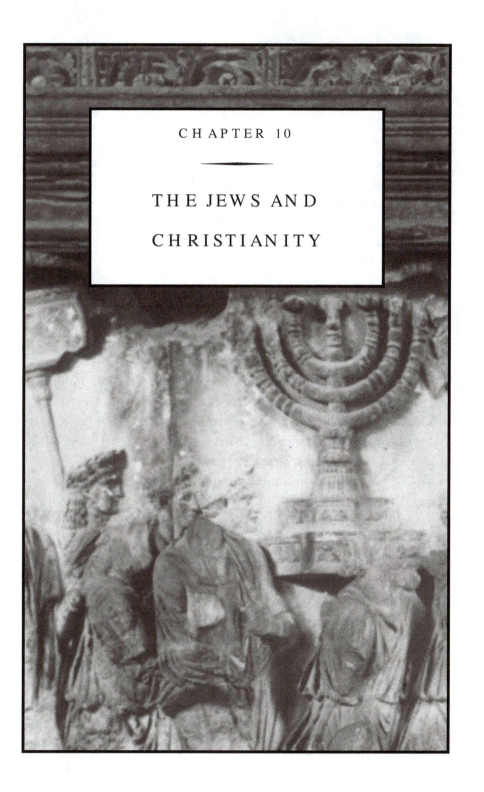

CHAPTER 10

———

THE JEWS AND

CHRISTIANITY

With the mind alone, the Jews conceive of only one god. They regard as impious those who fashion from perishable materials images of gods in the likeness of men. The supreme and eternal being is for them inimitable and eternal. Therefore they set up no statues in their cities, let alone in their temples. No flattery is paid to their kings, no honor to the Caesars [emperors]. (Tacitus, *Histories* 5.5)

We have seen how the state attempted to control the infiltration and adoption of foreign cults. A monotheistic religion, however, could not be reconciled with traditional Roman religious practice, as the above excerpt from Tacitus implies. The first extant reference to the presence of Jews in Rome is to their expulsion from the city in 139 BCE because they were trying to pass on their sacred rites to the Romans (Valerius Maximus, *Memorable Deeds and Words* 1.3.3). The numbers involved, however, were probably quite small, whether permanent residents or transients.

The sources for the next several decades are scanty, but by the late republic there was a substantial Jewish community permanently resident in Rome. Most of these people had been brought to Italy as captives, probably after Pompey's conquest of Syria in the 60s BCE. Many had been freed and later became Roman citizens (Philo, *Embassy to Gaius* 155). The Roman authorities were consequently faced with the permanent presence of people whose ancestral customs and conventions were very different from their own. The Jewish Sabbath, religious festivals, and dietary laws were incompatible with Roman civic life. Special dispensations were needed for Jews to have the rights to assemble for worship and pay the annual tax to the Temple in Jerusalem. The Jewish historian Flavius Josephus (37–ca. 100 CE) notes that Julius Caesar granted the Jews of Rome exemption from the ban on religious associations, nor did he prohibit them "from collecting contributions of money and holding common meals" (*Jewish Antiquities* 14.214). In 43 BCE the Roman commander in Asia Minor granted exemption from military service to the Jews living in that area.

> Alexander, son of Theodorus, ambassador of Hyrcanus, son of Alexander, the High Priest and Ethnarch of the Jews, has pointed out to me that his fellow Jews cannot undertake military service because they are not able to bear arms or march on the days of the sabbath. Nor can they obtain the traditional foodstuffs to which they are accustomed. I, therefore, like the governors before me, grant them exemption from military service and allow them to observe their native customs, to assemble for their sacred rites in accordance with their law, and to make contributions towards their sacrifices. I wish to inform the various cities of these things in writing. It is my wish that you write these instructions to the various cities. (Josephus, *Antiquities* 14.226–227)

Jewish communities had long been resident in the cities of the former Hellenistic kingdoms, extending from Greece to Egypt, from Asia Minor to Syria – areas that were all under Roman rule by the time of Augustus. That emperor granted exemptions, publicizing his benevolence in an inscription located on a prominent part of the temple of Rome and Augustus in Ancyra (modern Ankara, Turkey; Josephus, *Antiquities* 16.162–165). Philo, an Alexandrian Jew who went as ambassador to Rome in 38 CE, reminded the emperor Caligula of Augustus' consideration.

> Augustus knew that the Jews have places for prayer meetings and meet together in these places, especially on the holy sabbaths

when they come together as a group to learn their ancestral wisdom. He also knew that the Jews collect money for religious purposes from their first-fruits, sending this money to Jerusalem with people to offer the sacrifices. However, he did not banish them from Rome or deprive them of their Roman citizenship just because they were careful to maintain their identities as Jews. Nor did he take violent action against their houses of prayer. He did not forbid them to assemble to receive instruction in their laws, nor did he oppose their collection of the first-fruits. (Philo, *Embassy to Gaius* 156–157)

Tiberius, however, banished most of the Jews who were living in Rome because they were flocking there in great numbers and converting many Romans to their ways (Dio 57.18.5a). Of the four thousand Jews who were assigned to military service in Sardinia, many were punished for refusing to serve because they feared breaking the Jewish laws (Josephus, *Antiquities* 18.81–84). Tacitus and Suetonius connect the expulsion of Jews with the suppression of the worship of Isis, and Suetonius notes that astrologers were also banished (Tacitus, *Annals* 2.85; Suetonius, *Tiberius* 36). These expulsions are another example of opposition to foreign cults at a time of political instability.

Caligula, Tiberius' successor as emperor, encountered problems with the Jews of Alexandria. Relations between the Greek and the Jewish residents there had never been easy. The Greeks had long resented the right to self-government that the Jews had received under the Ptolemies and continued to hold under Roman rule. That resentment erupted in riots in 38 CE (Philo, *Against Flaccus* 54). The Roman governor unsuccessfully attempted to detain Philo's mission to Rome, where Caligula engaged in further delaying tactics. After Caligula's assassination in 41 CE, the new emperor, Claudius, wrote to the people of Alexandria urging them to adopt a more tolerant attitude toward the Jews, while also issuing stern warnings to the Jews (Greek Papyri in the British Museum 1912, lines 73–103; see Williams 1998: 133–134).

There were also problems in Judaea. Contrary to Tacitus' statement that all was quiet under Tiberius (*Histories* 5.9), the Roman procurator, Pontius Pilate, had to deal with local unrest among various Jewish sects and teachers, including Jesus. Caligula further outraged the Jews when he attempted to enforce the imperial cult in Judaea. In Jamnia, a coastal town with a mixed population of Greeks and Jews, the Greeks set up an altar, which the Jews immediately demolished. Caligula then decreed that the Temple in Jerusalem be converted into a shrine in his honor with an enormous statue of himself in the guise of Jupiter. Petronius, the governor of Syria, was sent to Judaea with military forces. He advised the Jews to take their time in constructing the statue, thus avoiding armed conflict. As in the case of Philo's mission, Caligula's death alleviated the situation, and the conversion of the Temple was abandoned.

At the beginning of his reign, Caligula's successor, Claudius, had problems with the Jewish population in Rome itself. He closed the synagogues but permitted the Jews to observe their traditional way of life, since "it would have been difficult to bar them from the city without causing immense disorder because of the numbers involved" (Dio 60.6.6). A few years later, however, there was an expulsion, "because the Jews were constantly causing disturbances at the instigation of one Chrestus" (Suetonius, *Claudius* 25). If Chrestus is identified with Jesus Christ, this would be the first reference in Greco-Roman literature to people for whom Jesus was the Messiah (the Christ). The New Testament *Acts of the Apostles* and letters of Paul to various Christian communities are evidence of the spread of Christianity during the late 30s and the 40s CE, indicating the likelihood that there were Christians in Rome during Claudius' reign (41–54 CE).

Tacitus, writing years later, reports the scapegoating of Christians after a fire in 64 CE. This is the first unambiguous reference in Greco-Roman literature to the presence in Rome of Christians, then probably regarded as one Jewish sect among many.

To suppress this rumor [of arson], Nero substituted as culprits and punished with cruel refinements those who were hated for

their wickedness and popularly known as Christians. The origi-
nator of their name, Christus, had been executed in the reign of
Tiberius by the procurator Pontius Pilate. The deadly supersti-
tion (*superstitio*) was checked for a time only to break out again,
not only in Judaea, the source of the evil, but even in the capital
itself. . . .

First self-acknowledged Christians were arrested. Then, on
their evidence, a large number were found guilty. . . . Their deaths
were made an object of mockery. Covered with the skins of wild
beasts, they were torn in pieces by dogs or fastened on crosses,
and, when daylight failed, they were set alight to serve as torches
by night. (Tacitus, *Annals* 15.44)

Two years later, trouble again erupted in Judaea between the Greeks
and Jews. The local authorities in the port city of Caesarea failed to
deal with the situation, protests broke out in Jerusalem, and the whole
province revolted. Nero sent Vespasian, one of his leading generals, to
put down the rebellion. After Nero's death, Vespasian was proclaimed
emperor and returned to Rome, leaving his son Titus to take Jerusalem
by siege. The Temple was destroyed, the Jewish council of the Sanhedrin
and the office of High Priest abolished, proselytizing forbidden, and the
tax previously paid to the Temple was henceforth to be paid to Jupiter
Capitolinus. Dio remarks that the Temple was destroyed on the Sabbath,
"a day that even now Jews reverence more than any other." Professed
Jews were to pay an annual tribute of two drachmas to Capitoline Jupiter.
Both Vespasian and Titus were hailed as *imperator* (commander-in-chief)
and received victory honors in Rome, including the construction of
triumphal arches (Dio 65.7.2).

After the suppression of this revolt, the literary sources show a prej-
udice against the Jews that is generally lacking in the era of the Julio-
Claudians, an intolerance that is also reflected in the attitude of the
Roman authorities. Suetonius recalls an instance of the persecution of
Jews during the reign of Domitian (81–96 CE).

78. Arch of Titus in the Roman Forum, built to commemorate the suppression of the Jewish Revolt and the taking of Jerusalem in 70 CE by the future emperor Titus.

79. Relief panel in the passage leading through the Arch of Titus. Soldiers, wearing laurel wreathes symbolizing victory, carry the spoils taken from the Temple in Jerusalem that were displayed in the triumphal procession in Rome. (*Left to right*) a menorah (seven-branched candlestick), the Table of the Bread of the Presence, and two trumpets.

80. Relief on the opposite panel inside the Arch of Titus: Titus is shown riding in the triumphal chariot, drawn by four horses and led by the goddess Roma. Behind him is the winged goddess, Victory.

Besides other taxes, that on the Jews was levied with the utmost rigor. Prosecutions were brought against those who either lived as Jews without acknowledging their faith or who concealed their origin and did not pay the tax imposed upon their race. I recall that as a young man I was present when a ninety-year-old man was physically examined before the procurator and a very crowded court, to see whether he was circumcised. (Suetonius, *Domitian* 12)

A second revolt in Judaea was brutally suppressed (132–135 CE), and the emperor Hadrian banned the entire Jewish nation from setting foot in the territory around Jerusalem. The city was colonized by Gentiles and renamed Aelia after Hadrian's family, and the province of Judaea became Palestina.

After the First Jewish Revolt, Christianity was increasingly regarded as a separate religion. What may well have been a widespread Roman perspective on Christianity is revealed by an exchange of correspondence

81. Coin commemorating the capture of Judaea (IUDAEA CAPTA): (*obv.*)
Vespasian wearing a laurel wreath; (*rev.*) the Roman victor is standing behind a
palm tree with a Jewish female captive seated at its foot, mourning.

in 112 CE between Pliny the Younger, the newly appointed governor of the province of Bithynia-Pontus (on the southern coast of the
Black Sea in modern Turkey), and the emperor Trajan. Since it was
Pliny's responsibility to decide whether or not a charge was deserv-
ing of punishment, he asks Trajan for advice about the policy to adopt
toward Christians against whom criminal allegations were being made.
From Pliny's account it is apparent that the spread of Christianity was
causing pagan temples to be deserted. From a Roman point of view,
such a failure to maintain the traditional worship of the gods (*cultus
deorum*) would have put the *pax deorum* in jeopardy. As with other
new cults or religions, there would also have been the fear of political
subversion.

The matter was treated as a potential crime, and Pliny describes in
detail the procedures he was using to test the alleged Christians, the most
crucial of which was a requirement to worship the emperor and other
Roman gods.

> I asked them directly if they were Christians. If they admitted
> it, I repeated the question a second and third time, threatening
> them with capital punishment. If they still persisted, I ordered
> them to be executed. . . .
>
> Those who denied that they were or ever had been Chris-
> tians, I thought should be released when they had repeated after

me an invocation to the gods and made a supplication of incense and wine to your image which I had ordered to be placed for this purpose with the statues of the gods. They had also cursed Christ. All these are actions that those who are true Christians, so it is said, cannot be forced to do. (Pliny the Younger, *Letters* 10.96)

The emperor's rescript, a response that had the authority of law, is preserved among Pliny's letters. Trajan was insistent that Christians were not to be sought out; each case was to be tried on an individual basis. The penalty for those who persisted in confessing their faith was death, but pardon was ensured by repentance and proof of that repentance by worshiping the Roman gods. The emperor's reply concludes with the instruction that "anonymous pamphlets should have no place in a criminal proceeding, as it is a most dangerous precedent and not in keeping with the spirit of our age" (Pliny the Younger, *Letters* 10.97).

The story of persecutions, followed by the acceptance and later the establishment of Christianity, belongs to another volume. This introduction to Roman religion is perhaps best concluded with an excerpt from a petition of Symmachus, the pagan prefect of Rome, who wrote to the emperor Valentinian II in 384 CE asking him to restore the pagan altar of Victory, previously removed from the Senate house by the emperor Gratian. This letter makes a plea for magnanimity, while also reflecting the distinctive features of traditional Roman religion.

Every man has his own way of life (*mos*) and his own religious practices (*ritus*). Similarly, the divine mind has given to different cities different religious rites (*cultus*) that protect them. As souls are apportioned to men at birth, so, too, does each nation receive a Genius, which guides its destiny. In addition there is also the bestowal of favors (*utilitas*) which, more than anything else, proves to man the existence of the gods. Since all human reasoning is obscure on this matter, from where else does knowledge of the gods more correctly come than from the recollection and evidence of success? If the long passage of time gives authority to religious rites, we must keep faith with so many centuries and follow our fathers, who followed their fathers and consequently prospered.

Let us imagine that Rome herself is standing here now and addressing these words to you: "Best of emperors, fathers of the fatherland, respect the number of years that the dutiful (*pius*) performance of religious rites has brought to me. Let me enjoy the ancient ceremonies, for I do not regret them. Let me live according to my own custom (*mos*), for I am free. This is the worship (*cultus*) which made the whole world obedient to my laws. These are the rituals (*sacra*) which drove back Hannibal from my walls and the Senones [a Gallic tribe] from my Capitol. Have I been preserved only to be criticized in my old age? I will consider the changes that people think must be instituted, but correction in old age is insulting and too late."

And so we are asking for amnesty (*pax*) for the gods of our fathers, our native gods. It is reasonable to assume that whatever each of us worships is one and the same. We look up at the same stars, the same sky is common to us all, the same universe encompasses us. What difference does it make which system each of us uses to seek the truth? It is not by just one route that man can arrive at so great a mystery. (Symmachus, *Dispatches to the Emperor* 3.8–10)

# CHRONOLOGY

---

46   Julius Caesar's reform of the calendar
44   Assassination of Julius Caesar
31   Battle of Actium, defeat of Antony and Cleopatra
27   Octavian takes the title Augustus

*CE*

14   Tiberius becomes emperor
19   Suppression of the cult of Isis, and expulsion of Jews from Rome
37   Caligula becomes emperor
41   Claudius becomes emperor
43   Temple of Isis dedicated in Campus Martius
c. 49   Claudius' expulsion of Jews from Rome
54   Nero becomes emperor
64   Christians made scapegoats after the fire of Rome
66–73   First Jewish Revolt
70   Titus sacks Jerusalem
111   Pliny's letter from Bithynia regarding Christians, and Trajan's rescript
133   Second Jewish Revolt
135   Defeat of revolt, expulsion of Jews from Jerusalem, Judaea made part of Syria Palestina

# MAPS

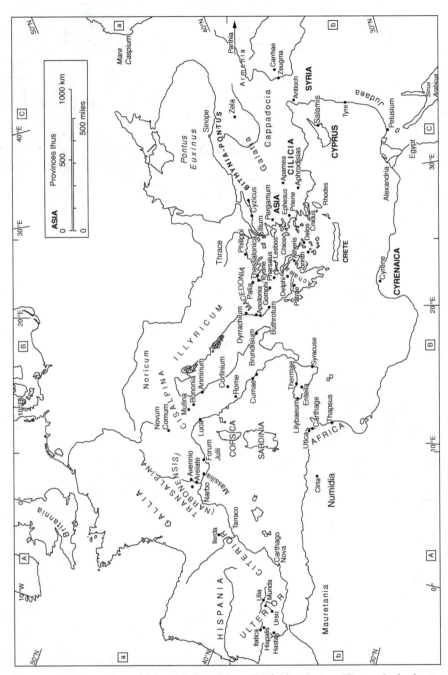

Map 1. The Roman world in 50 BCE. From *Cambridge Ancient History*, 2nd ed. (*CAH*), vol. 9, p. 566, map 14.

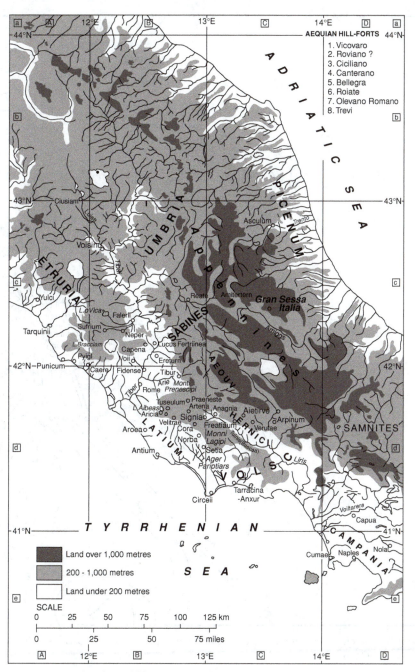

**AEQUIAN HILL-FORTS**

1. Vicovaro
2. Roviano ?
3. Ciciliano
4. Canterano
5. Bellegra
6. Roiate
7. Olevano Romano
8. Trevi

Land over 1,000 metres

200 - 1,000 metres

Land under 200 metres

SCALE

| 0 | 25 | 50 | 75 | 100 | 125 km |

| 0 | 25 | 50 | 75 miles |

Map 2. Central Italy in fifth century BCE. From *CAH,* vol. 7, pt. 2, p. 283, map 3.

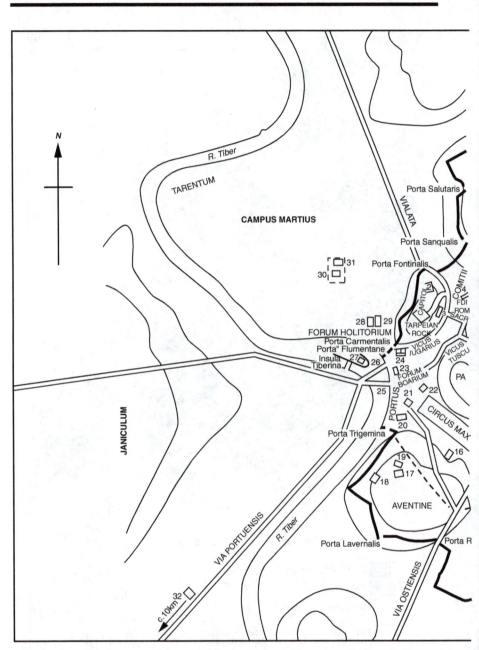

Map 3. The city of Rome in the early third century BCE. From *CAH*, vol. 7, part 2, pp. 406–407, fig. 10.

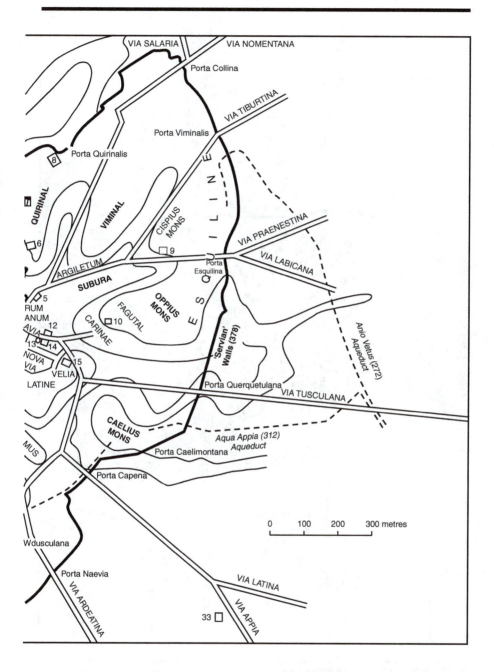

VIA SALARIA
VIA NOMENTANA
Porta Collina
VIA TIBURTINA
Porta Viminalis
Porta Quirinalis
8
7
QUIRINAL
VIMINAL
CISPIUS MONS
ESQUILINE
N
9
VIA PRAENESTINA
Porta Esquilina
VIA LABICANA
ARGILETUM
6
SUBURA
RUM ANUM
5
AVIA
12
13 14
NOVA VIA
LATINE
VELIA
15
FAGUTAL
OPPIUS MONS
CARINAE
10
'Servian' Walls (378)
Anio Vetus (272) Aqueduct
Porta Querquetulana
VIA TUSCULANA
CAELIUS MONS
Aqua Appia (312) Aqueduct
Porta Caelimontana
Porta Capena
MUS

0    100    200    300 metres

Wdusculana
Porta Naevia
VIA ARDEATINA
VIA LATINA
VIA APPIA
33

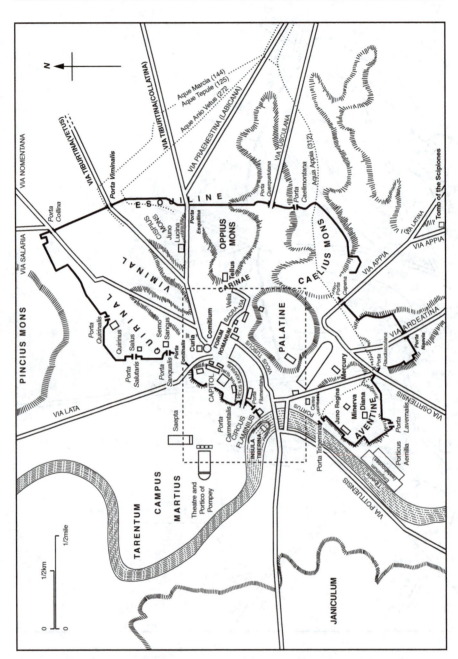

Map 4. (a) Rome in the last two centuries of the Republic. From *CAH*, vol. 9, p. 70.

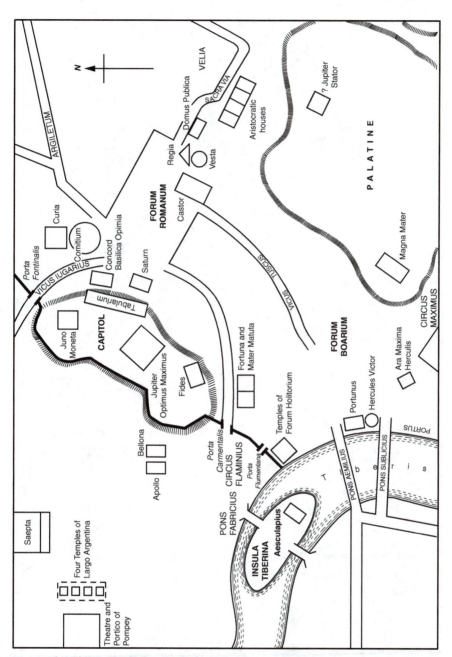

Map 4. (b) The Capitol, Forum, and Palatine area in the last two centuries of the Republic. From *CAH*, vol. 9, p. 71.

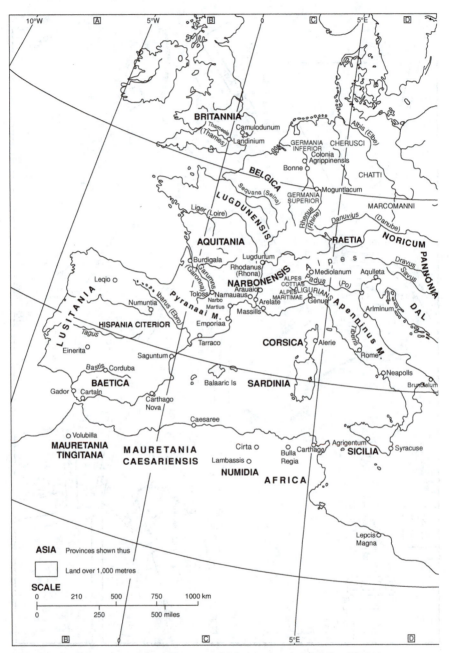

Map 5. The Roman world in the time of Augustus and the Julio-Christian emperors. From *CAH*, vol. 10, map 1.

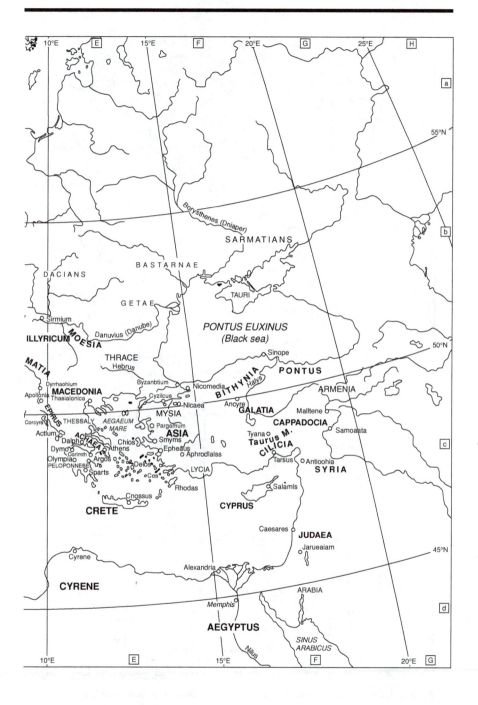

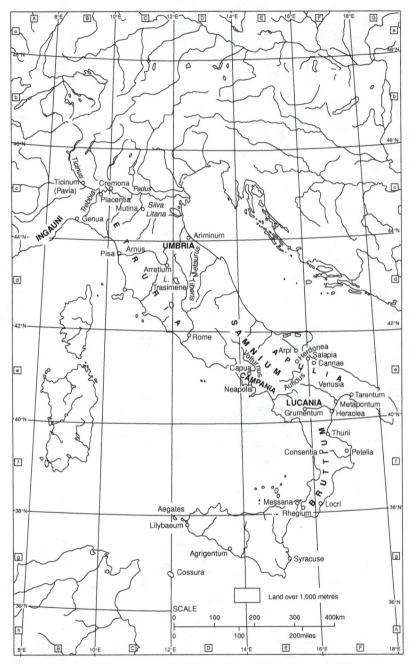

Map 6. Italy and Sicily during the Second Punic War. From *CAH*, vol. 8, p. 48, map 8.

# GODS

---

Aesculapius: God of healing, the Greek Asclepius.

Apollo: Originally a Greek god, son of Zeus and Leto (Roman Latona).

Bacchus, also known as Dionysus: Greek god, son of Zeus and Semele, who was worshiped in Rome as Liber Pater in the early fifth century. His cult involved initiation.

Ceres: Ancient Italo-Roman goddess of growth, often identified with the Greek Demeter.

Cybele or Cybebe: Anatolian mother goddess, imported to Rome and worshiped as Magna Mater, the Great Mother. Her consort was Attis, and her eunuch priests were called Galli.

Diana: Italian goddess, often identified with Artemis, sister of Apollo and daughter of Zeus and Leto.

Janus: God of doors and gates, openings and beginnings, represented as simultaneously facing in two directions.

Juno: Ancient Italic deity. Also worshiped as Juno Regina (Queen), Juno Sospita (Protector), and Juno Lucina (of childbirth).

Jupiter: Preeminent Roman deity often identified with the Greek Zeus. Worshiped on the Capitoline Hill as Jupiter Optimus Maximus in a temple shared with Juno and Minerva.

Isis: Egyptian goddess whose cult infiltrated Rome and Italy in the early first century BCE.

Magna Mater: Great Mother. *See* Cybele.

Mars: Originally an Italic god of vegetation, soon associated with war, and so merged with the Greek war-god Ares.

Mercury: Patron of trade and commerce. Probably Italic, though later merged with the Greek Hermes.

Minerva: Italic goddess of handicrafts, often identified with Athena, daughter of Zeus.

Mithras: Ancient Indo-Iranian god whose worship was widespread in the Roman Empire, especially among the lower ranks of the military.

Neptune: Italic god of water, later assimilated to the Greek Poseidon.

Quirinus: Probably of Sabine origin, later associated with the deified Romulus.

Saturn: Thought by some to be an Italic god of sowing or seed corn. Others consider him Etruscan.

Venus: Goddess of sexual desire, often identified with the Greek Aphrodite.

Vesta: Goddess of the hearth, not anthropomorphized, worshiped as a perpetual flame in the Forum.

Vulcan: Ancient Roman god of destructive and volcanic fire. The Greek equivalent was Hephaestus.

# GLOSSARY

aedile: Minor elected official or magistrate.

augurs: Official Roman diviners and priests who held office for life and were members of the augural college.

augury: Form of divination used by augurs to ascertain whether a proposed course of state action had divine approval.

auspices (*auspicia*): Literally the observation of birds, but more widely applied to a variety of signs thought to have been sent by the gods as an indication of their favor or disfavor. As opposed to augury, auspices only pertained to one day and were taken before any state action was initiated.

Aventine: One of the seven hills of Rome.

*camillus* (fem. *camilla*): Attendant, usually below the age of puberty, of a priest.

consuls: The two chief magistrates of Rome during the republic, who were elected annually to hold civic and military power (*imperium*).

decemvirs: *See* quindecimvirs.

denarius (pl. denarii): Roman silver coin.

dictator: Official appointed for six months to deal with a particular emergency. Held supreme military and judicial power even though other magistrates remained in office.

divination: Interpretation of signs or messages believed to have been sent by the gods. These signs – auspices, portents, prodigies, dreams, and prophecies – were interpreted by augurs, *haruspices,* or by quindecimvirs.

Etruscans: Non–Indo-European-speaking peoples living north of Rome in Etruria.

expiation: An action intended to make amends or atonement for a perceived offense against the gods.

*fas:* An action that is lawful in the eyes of the gods, as opposed to *nefas* (an impiety).

fetials (*fetiales*): Priests whose duties were the making of treaties and the declaration of war.

*flamines* (sing. *flamen*): Priests, one who served Jupiter (*flamen Dialis*), another Mars, and a third Quirinus.

*Galli* (sing. *Gallus*): Eunuch priests of Cybele (Magna Mater).

Genius: A divine "double" of an individual, usually a male.

Hannibal: A Carthaginian general (247–183 BCE) who invaded Italy in 218 BCE, defeating the Romans at Trasimene and Cannae. He was eventually defeated in 202 BCE at the battle of Zama in North Africa.

*haruspices* (sing. *haruspex*): Diviners who originally came from Etruria.

*Lar* (pl. *Lares*): The spirit or deity that guarded and protected a household and its members.

Laws of the Twelve Tables: A collection of statutes traditionally dated c. 450 BCE. The foundation of Roman law.

*lectisternium:* A banquet in honor of the gods at which their statues were placed on draped couches outside the temples, and food set before them.

libation: Liquid offering to the gods, usually of wine.

*lituus:* A staff, curved at the top, the symbol of an augur.

*manes:* Spirits, or shades, of the dead.

*nefas:* An action that was unlawful in the eyes of the gods, an impiety.

*numen* (pl. *numina*): Divine power(s).

Octavian: Great-nephew of Julius Caesar, adopted as his son, who took the title Gaius Julius Caesar Octavianus. In 27 BCE, Octavian took the name Augustus.

oracle: A divine utterance, or prophecy, made by a god through a priest or priestess. The word can also apply to the priest or priestess making the utterance.

Palatine: One of the seven hills of Rome.

*patera:* A shallow bowl or dish used for pouring liquid libations.

*paterfamilias:* Male head of a family, usually a father or grandfather.

*pax deorum:* The favor or benevolence (literally, the peace, as opposed to the anger, *ira*) of the gods.

*Penates:* Household gods that protected the pantry or stores-cupboard.

plebeians or plebs: The less privileged group of Roman citizens, in contrast to the patricians.

*pomerium:* Sacred boundary of the city of Rome.

*pontifex* (pl. *pontifices*): Official priest of the state who held office for life and was an interpreter of ritual matters, including flaws in their performance.

portent: A strange or unusual occurrence thought to have been sent by the gods as an indication of a future event. A portent could become a prodigy only if so decreed by state authorities. *See* prodigy.

praetor: An elected official.

prodigy: The term "prodigy" (*prodigium*) should refer strictly to a portent that has been accepted by the state authorities as indicating that the *pax deorum* has been broken.

quindecimvirs: Board of priests in charge of the performance of ritual. Also guardians of the Sibylline Books. Their number was increased from two to ten to fifteen (thus *quindecimviri*) and, finally, to sixteen.

*religio:* According to the *Oxford Latin Dictionary* (1982), a "sense of the presence of supernatural power, religious fear, awe" or "religious feeling." *Religio* also implies a sense of obligation. Note, however, that the translation will vary according to context.

Senate: Body, consisting chiefly of ex-magistrates, whose chief function was to give advice to the magistrates on matters of domestic and foreign policy, finance, and religion.

Sibylline Books: A collection of oracles kept in the temple of Jupiter on the Capitoline and later transferred by Augustus to the Palatine temple of Apollo.

*supplicatio:* Ritual of collective prayer to propitiate the gods, performed on behalf of the citizen body, at times of crisis or in preparation for war.

toga: An undyed woolen robe, the distinctive dress of adult male Roman citizens.

triumph: Victory parade granted by the Senate to a general who was judged to have won an outstanding victory against a non-Roman enemy.

*vitium:* A flaw or error in the performance of a prayer, sacrifice, or in the sacrificial victim itself.

votive offering: A gift given to a god in payment of a vow, as a thank-offering for the granting of a request.

# ANCIENT SOURCES

---

Most of the sources referred to in this volume are available in the Loeb Classical Library and the Penguin translation series.

Apuleius (c. 125–c. 170 CE): Author of the novel *Metamorphoses* (also known as *The Golden Ass*).

Cato the Elder (234–149 BCE): Author of *On Agriculture*.

Catullus (c. 84–54 BCE): Roman poet.

Cicero (106–43 BCE): Orator, politician, writer of letters and philosophy and treatises including *On the Nature of the Gods* and *On Divination*.

Dio, Cassius Dio (c. 160–c. 235 CE): Greek who wrote a history of Rome.

Dionysius of Halicarnassus: Greek resident of Rome from 30 to 8 BCE. Author of *Roman Antiquities,* a detailed account of Rome's early history.

Festus (late second century CE): Abridged early-first-century CE work *On the Significance of Words*.

Gellius, Aulus Gellius (c. 123–c. 180 CE): Author of *Attic Nights,* essays that include quotations from earlier authors whose works are otherwise lost.

Horace (65–8 BCE): Lyric poet and satirist.

Josephus (37–c. 100 CE): Jewish captive in Rome; author of *Jewish War* and *Jewish Antiquities.*

Juvenal (late first and early second centuries CE): Satirist of Roman follies and vices.

Laws of the Twelve Tables: A collection of statutes, traditionally codified c. 450 CE; the foundation of Roman law.

Livy (c. 59 BCE–17 CE): Author of a history of Rome from its foundation to his own times. Of the one hundred and forty-two books, thirty-five have survived.

Lucretius (c. 94–55 or 51 BCE): Author of poem, *On the Nature of Things,* concerning Epicurean philosophy.

Macrobius (c. 400 CE): Author of *Saturnalia Conversations.*

Martial (c. 40–104 CE): Poet, wrote epigrams.

Ovid (43 BCE–17 CE): Author of love poetry, the mythological epic *Metamorphoses,* and *Fasti,* which concerns festivals of the first six months of the year.

Petronius (d. 66 CE): Author of the novel *Satyricon.*

Philo (c. 30 BCE–45 CE): Philosopher and political writer, a leading exponent of Alexandrian-Jewish culture.

Plautus (c. 254–184 BCE): Latin playwright.

Pliny the Elder (23/24–79 CE): Author of *Natural History,* an encyclopaedia of contemporary knowledge.

Pliny the Younger (61/62–c. 112 CE): Nephew of Pliny the Elder. Pursued a political career and published his own correspondence.

Plutarch (c. 46–died after 120 CE): Greek philosopher, author of parallel lives of prominent Greeks and Romans, and *Roman Questions.*

Polybius (c. 200–c. 118 BCE): A Greek who wrote a history of Rome's rise to world power in the late third and first half of the second century BCE.

Seneca the Younger (c. 4 BCE–65 CE): Stoic philosopher.

Statius (c. 45–96 CE): Poet, author of a collection of miscellaneous poems entitled *Silvae.*

Suetonius (c. 69–c. 130 CE): Biographer of Julius Caesar and of the first eleven emperors.

Symmachus (c. 340–402 CE): Orator, ardent supporter of traditional Roman religion.

Tacitus (c. 55–118 CE): Historian and author of *Annals* and *Histories.*

Terence (d. c. 159 BCE): Latin playwright.

Valerius Maximus: During the reign of Tiberius (14–37 CE), he wrote *Memorable Words and Deeds,* a collection of anecdotes illustrating human character.

Varro (116–27 BCE): Author of *Human and Divine Antiquities,* which survives only in excerpts quoted by other authors.

Virgil (70–19 BCE): Poet whose major work, *The Aeneid,* tells of Aeneas' journey from Troy to Italy.

# BIBLIOGRAPHY

## GENERAL REFERENCE WORKS

Adkins, Lesley, and Roy A. Adkins. 2000. *Dictionary of Roman Religion.* New York: Oxford University Press.

Boatwright, Mary T., Daniel J. Gargola, and Richard J. A. Talbert. 2004. *The Romans and Their History: From Village to Empire.* New York: Oxford University Press.

Beard, Mary, John North, and Simon Price. 1998. *Religions of Rome:* Vol. 1, *A History;* Vol. 2, *A Sourcebook.* Cambridge: Cambridge University Press. Cited as *BNP.*

*Corpus Inscriptionum Latinarum.* 1863–. Berlin. Cited as *CIL.*

Dessau, H. 1962–. *Inscriptiones Latinae Selectae.* Berlin. Cited as *ILS.*

Hornblower, Simon, and Antony Spawforth, eds. 2003. *Oxford Classical Dictionary,* rev. 3rd ed. Oxford and New York: Oxford University Press.

## FURTHER READING

Ando, Clifford, ed. 2003. *Roman Religion.* Edinburgh: Edinburgh University Press.

Barton, Tamsyn. 1994. *Ancient Astrology.* London and New York: Routledge.

Davies, Jason P. 2004. *Rome's Religious History: Livy, Tacitus and Ammianus on Their Gods*. Cambridge: Cambridge University Press.

Dickie, Matthew. 2001. *Magic and Magicians in the Greco-Roman World*. London and New York: Routledge.

Dowden, Ken. 1995. *Religion and the Romans*. London: Bristol Classical Press.

Dunbabin, K. M. D. 1978. *The Mosaics of Roman North Africa: Studies in Iconography and Patronage*. Oxford: Clarendon Press; New York: Oxford University Press.

Faraone, Christopher A. 2003. "When Spells Worked Magic." *Archaeology* 56.2:48–52.

Foss, Pedar. 1997. "Watchful Lares: Roman Household Organization and the Rituals of Cooking and Dining." In *Domestic Space in the Roman World: Pompeii and Beyond*, ed. Ray Laurence and Andrew Wallace-Hadrill (= *Journal of Roman Archaeology*, Suppl. 22, Portsmouth, RI), pp. 196–218.

Gager, John G. 1992. *Curse Tablets and Binding Spells from the Ancient World*. New York: Oxford University Press.

Graf, Fritz. 1997. *Magic in the Ancient World*. Cambridge, MA: Harvard University Press.

Hope, Valerie. 1997. "A Roof over the Dead: Communal Tombs and Family Structure." In *Domestic Space in the Roman World: Pompeii and Beyond*, ed. Ray Laurence and Andrew Wallace-Hadrill (= *Journal of Roman Archaeology*, Suppl. 22, Portsmouth, RI), pp. 69–88.

Linderski, J. 1995. "Roman Religion in Livy." In *Roman Questions: Selected Papers*. Stuttgart: F. Steiner, pp. 608–625.

Mantle, I. C. 2002. "The Roles of Children in Roman Religion." *Greece and Rome* 49:85–106.

Ogden, D. 2002. *Magic, Witchcraft and Ghosts in the Greek and Roman Worlds: A Sourcebook*. Oxford and New York: Oxford University Press.

Orlin, Eric M. 1997. *Temples, Religion and Politics in the Roman Republic*. Leiden: E. J. Brill.

Parker, Holt. 2004. "Why Were the Vestals Virgins? Or the Chastity of Women and the Safety of the Roman State." *American Journal of Philology* 125:563–601.

Patterson, John R. 2000. "Living and Dying in the City of Rome: Houses and Tombs." In *Ancient Rome: The Archaeology of the Eternal City,* ed. Jon Coulston and Hazel Dodge. Oxford: Oxford School of Archaeology, pp. 259–288.

Price, S. R. F. 1984. *Rituals and Power: The Roman Imperial Cult in Asia Minor.* Cambridge: Cambridge University Press.

Ryberg, I. S. 1955. "Rites of the State Religion in Roman Art." *Memoirs of the American Academy in Rome* 22.

Scheid, John. 2003. *An Introduction to Roman Religion.* Translated by Janet Lloyd. Bloomington: Indiana University Press.

Scullard, H. H. 1981. *Festivals and Ceremonies of the Roman Republic.* Ithaca, NY: Cornell University Press.

Treggiari, Susan M. 1991. *Roman Marriage.* Oxford: Clarendon Press; New York: Oxford University Press.

    2002. *Roman Social History.* London and New York: Routledge.

Turcan, Robert. 2000. *The Gods of Ancient Rome.* Translated by Antonia Nevill. Edinburgh: Edinburgh University Press.

Warrior, Valerie M. 2002. *Roman Religion: A Sourcebook.* Newburyport, MA: Focus Press.

Williams, Margaret. 1998. *The Jews among the Greeks and Romans: A Diasporan Sourcebook.* Baltimore, MD: Johns Hopkins University Press.

Zanker, Paul. 1988. *The Power of Images in the Age of Augustus.* Ann Arbor: University of Michigan Press.

# ILLUSTRATION CREDITS

1  Kathleen M. Coleman
2  (a) Scala / Art Resource, NY. (b) Valerie M. Warrior
3  Ann Koloski-Ostrow
4  Deutsches Archäologisches Institut, Rome
5  Hampden Maps, London
6  Valerie M. Warrior
7  Courtesy of the Trustees of the British Museum, London
8  Scala / Art Resource, NY
9  Deutsches Archäologisches Institut, Rome
10  Scala / Art Resource, NY
11  Bridgeman-Giraudon / Erich Lessing / Art Resource, NY
12  Deutsches Archäologisches Institut, Rome
13  Alinari / Art Resource, NY
14  Photo: Ch. Thioc. Courtesy of Musée de la civilisation gallo-romaine, Lyon, France
15  Alinari / Art Resource, NY
16  Deutsches Archäologisches Institut, Rome
17  Réunion des Musées Nationaux / Art Resource, NY
18  Deutsches Archäologisches Institut, Rome
19  Courtesy of the Trustees of the British Museum

20  Alinari / Art Resource, NY
21  Deutsches Archäologisches Institut, Rome
22  Alinari / Art Resource, NY
23  Werner Forman Archive / Art Resource, NY
24  Scala / Art Resource, NY
25  Alinari / Art Resource, NY
26  Erich Lessing / Art Resource, NY
27  Réunion des Musées Nationaux / Art Resource, NY
28  Erich Lessing / Art Resource, NY
29  Archivio Fotografico della Soprintendenza per i beni archeologici di Ostia, inv. R. 4530. Photo: De Antonis
30  Archivio Fotografico della Soprintendenza per i beni archeologici di Ostia, inv. D. 3901. Photo: De Antonis
31  Courtesy of the Trustees of the British Museum
32  Scala / Art Resource, NY
33  Alinari / Art Resource, NY
34  Deutsches Archäologisches Institut, Rome
35  Valerie M. Warrior
36  Valerie M. Warrior
37  Courtesy of the Trustees of the British Museum
38  M. and P. Chuzeville. Réunion des Musées Nationaux / Art Resource, NY
39  Scala / Art Resource, NY
40  Deutsches Archäologisches Institut, Rome
41  Vanni / Art Resource, NY
42  Courtesy of the Trustees of the British Museum, London
43  Valerie M. Warrior
44  (*left*) Deutsches Archäologisches Institut, Rome. (*right*) Alinari / Art Resource, NY
45  Deutsches Archäologisches Institut, Rome
46  Réunion des Musées Nationaux / Art Resource, NY
47  Kathleen M. Coleman
48  Deutsches Archäologisches Institut, Rome

49 Scala / Art Resource, NY

50 Gérard Blot. Réunion des Musées Nationaux / Art Resource, NY

51 Erich Lessing / Art Resource, NY

52 Scala / Art Resource, NY

53 Metropolitan Museum of Art, gift of Henry G. Marquand, 1897 (97.22.24). Photo: Metropolitan Museum, 184012 B

54 Deutsches Archäologisches Institut, Rome

55 Réunion des Musées Nationaux / Art Resource, NY

56 Scala / Art Resource, NY

57 Kunsthistorisches Museum, Vienna

58 AKG

59 Erich Lessing / Art Resource, NY

60 Alinari / Art Resource, NY

61 Scala / Werner Forman Archive / Art Resource, NY

62 Deutsches Archäologisches Institut, Rome

63 Erich Lessing / Art Resource, NY

64 Roger Wood / Corbis

65 Scanned from R. Wünsch, *Sethianische Verfluchungstafeln aus Rom* (Leipzig: Teubner, 1898), p. 16

66 Courtesy of the Papyrus Collection of the Institut für Altertumskunde of the University of Cologne

67 Herve Lewandowski. Réunion des Musées Nationaux / Art Resource, NY

68 Courtesy of the Visitors of the Ashmolean Museum

69 Courtesy of the Visitors of the Ashmolean Museum

70 Scala / Art Resource, NY

71 Alinari / Art Resource, NY

72 Scala / Art Resource, NY

73 Scala / Art Resource, NY

74 Erich Lessing / Art Resource, NY

75 Vienna Kunsthistorisches Museum

76 Scala / Art Resource, NY

77 Deutsches Archäologisches Institut, Rome

# INDEX